LIPSTICK ON A PIG

WHY BAIL-OUTS FAIL AND PEOPLE POWER WILL SUCCEED

Simon Deane-Johns
'The Pragmatist'

Searching
finance

First published 2012 by Searching Finance Ltd, 8 Whitehall Road, London W7 2JE, UK

ISBN: 978-1-907720-39-0

Typeset by: Deirdré Gyenes

LIPSTICK ON A PIG

WHY BAIL-OUTS FAIL AND PEOPLE POWER WILL SUCCEED

Simon Deane-Johns
'The Pragmatist'

About the author

Simon Deane-Johns is a practising lawyer who has qualified in England, New York State and Australia. He specialises in the law related to online retail financial services, e-commerce and information technology. He lives in west London with his wife and two children.

Having graduated from Sydney University with an Arts/Law degree, Simon began his career as a barrister in Sydney in 1990 and moved to London in 1994. Since then he has worked in the legal departments of Reuters, GE and Amazon.com. He was also an Associate at Dibb Lupton Alsop (now DLA Piper) from 1997 to 1999. From 1999 until 2001, Simon was a director and General Counsel of Earthport plc, one of the first e-wallet payment service providers. In 2004 he co-founded Zopa, the world's first person-to-person lending marketplace, where he remained General Counsel until 2008. Since 2005, Simon has worked as a consultant lawyer. He has advised on the creation of many new online e-commerce and financial services, and his clients include e-money issuers, payment service providers and peer-to-peer finance platforms.

Simon has been a member of the media board at the Society for Computers and Law since 2001 and is a member of the Interoperability Board of 'midata', a voluntary programme in which the UK Government is working with the private sector to give consumers increasing access to their personal data in a portable, electronic format.

Simon has spoken and written widely on e-commerce and financial services since 1997. Topics have included the role of social media in financial services, internet regulation, identity, behavioural targeting of internet advertising, the future of money and the reform of financial regulation. Simon began writing consistently about consumer empowerment on his blog 'Pragmatist' in 2007. He added a second blog, 'The Fine Print', in 2011 as a home for his thoughts on the law and legal practice.

Somehow, Simon finds the time to train for an annual 'Rowers' Revenge' triathlon and to coach mini-rugby at Wasps. In early July he can generally be found near a certain tree in Henley-on-Thames.

About Searching Finance

Searching Finance Ltd is a dynamic new voice in knowledge provision for the financial services and related professional sectors. Our mission is to provide expert, highly relevant and actionable information and analysis, written by professionals, for professionals. For more information, please visit www.searchingfinance.com

CONTENTS

ACKNOWLEDGEMENTS

Having peddled a few crime fiction manuscripts around literary agents in the '90s to no avail, I greeted Ashwin Rattan's offer to publish something based on the Pragmatist blog with a heady mixture of joy and scepticism. But I can honestly say that, from Ash's first tweet in June, he and his Searching Finance colleagues, Nigel Carn and Ann Tierney, could not have made the process any easier or more pleasurable, for which I am hugely grateful. Theirs is the future model of publishing.

That's not to say it's been easy to produce a coherent book from a collection of random blog posts scattered across four years. That process has had a major impact on family life over the past four months, not to mention the kitchen table. So, virtually all my thanks must go to my supremely patient, forgiving and supportive wife, Solveig, and our two children, Amber and Hunter. This book is dedicated to them.

I say virtually all my thanks, because there are squadrons of people who have my deep gratitude for contributing to and influencing the thoughts recorded here. Space and time don't allow me to name you all, but the following people deserve a special mention, in chronological order of their involvement:

- Adrian Deane-Johns, author and ex-adman, who enthusiastically transmitted to me his love of language and literature, suggesting I read Tom Wolfe's inspirational anthology 'The New Journalism' at age 10 and for providing endless encouragement and inspiration ever since;

- Tom Glocer, then General Counsel of Reuters America, for his offer to join the Reuters legal department in New York, and for handing out copies of 'Being Digital';
- The London partners of what was then Dibb Lupton Alsop, who decided they needed a lawyer who understood 'information services' and allowed me to grow that focus to include 'e-commerce';
- My executive colleagues at Earthport and GE, from whom I learned the value of starting every project with the customer;
- Glen Davis QC, who invited me to join the media board of the Society for Computers and Law, my board colleagues for welcoming my input, and to Laurence Eastham for his encouragement on the writing front;
- The Zopa team, and especially James Alexander, Dave Nicholson, Giles Andrews, Tim Parlett, Sarah Matthews and Linda Young for welcoming legal input into the design and implementation of the first P2P lending marketplace and for backing their lawyer through thick and thin and the self-confidence that inspired – and of course special thanks to the late Richard Duvall, who I hope would have been proud; and
- Mark Nepstad, Chris Marsden, Ian Brown, Lilian Edwards, Bruce Davis, Simon Clark, Bill James, Chris Skinner, Dave Birch, Cosmo Lush and Ash Rattan himself have all provided great opportunities in their own time to discuss the issues covered here.

Simon Deane-Johns
London
December 2011

INTRODUCTION

This series of books charts my irreverent attempts, via the 'Pragmatist' blog, to understand how we, as individuals, are able to personalise the one-size-fits-all existence traditionally offered by our institutions.

Over the series I'll consider the impact of this trend on our financial system, politics, unions, the church and beyond.

Why start with our financial system? Because, like it or not – and I believe that recent impromptu campsites demonstrate that most of us do *not* like it – our financial system is supposed to be the beating heart of our society, yet it's badly broken. And all the money we allocate to the existing structure is just so much lipstick on a pig. Greed and stupidity are winning. Keynes himself surely would have dropped by the campsite at St Paul's Cathedral:

> "When the accumulation of wealth is no longer of high social importance, there will be great changes in the code of morals. We shall be able to rid ourselves of many of the pseudo-moral principles which have hag-ridden us for two hundred years, by which we have exalted some of the most distasteful of human qualities into the position of the highest virtues."[1]

Yet there is hope, even in the face of financial doom. The 'occupations' are a sign that the majority of us have rounded the 'change curve'. Those unhappy campers would not have pitched their tents in our financial districts had they not instinctively sensed that *we all understand why they are there*. We all accept

1

the world has changed for the worse, and that something must be done. As we'll see, our shared sense of frustration with greed and concerns about sustainability are fuelling collaborative efforts through the social media to fundamentally change society for the better.

In theory, everyone should be interested in this book. But I suspect you'll read it only if you are interested in achieving greater control over your own existence, or because you intend facilitating that process for others. Or because you enjoy a good revolution.

But why would a *lawyer* write such a book – or the blog on which it's based?

Let's take a few steps back.

In 1996, I read 'Being Digital' by Nicholas Negroponte of MIT.[2] He reckoned the power of digital technology would only be fully realised when the technology itself disappeared from view – when the 'atoms' that make up the gadgets turned into the 'bits' that convey content, which in turn could be customised to personal taste. That struck me not so much as 'true' but as a very likely evolutionary trend. As a barrister in Sydney from 1990 to 1994, I'd learned to touch-type and edit my own documents, but was annoyed to have to learn a second language just to make my laptop speak English. It seemed obvious that this technology would need to become more usable. But who would facilitate that, and how – or why? By the time I read 'Being Digital', I was working in the New York legal department of Reuters, the world's largest supplier of news and financial information. Apart from supplying news, Reuters had been at the forefront of developing computer programmes, systems and networks within the financial markets for decades. But it didn't like the democratising influence of the internet. eBay and Amazon.com had been online for about a year, and the term 'e-commerce' was being widely used in the US, though not in the UK where Reuters was headquartered (Amazon.co.uk would not launch until 1998). Yet the major media were jealously guarding their content and allowed very little to be published electronically. Reuters itself was notoriously paranoid about the impact of the internet on its business model – in the summer of '96, I flew down to Dulles, Virginia, to negotiate a deal to supply AOL subscribers with merely the *top ten headlines of the day.*

A year later, as Reuters America ran into a pay and headcount freeze, I was asked to join the London office of DLA, the law firm, to advise large corporate clients on 'information services'. Luckily for my marketing push, it was a matter of weeks before the *Financial Times* began using the term 'e-commerce'.

Yet, while 'bits' had begun flowing in earnest amongst computers, the first wave of e-commerce was one-dimensional. Apart from sending emails, you could really only buy or read stuff on web sites. Real interaction was just a pipe-dream. Few senior executives (or law firm partners) really understood what was happening, or the potential that e-commerce held. When Egg launched its 'internet' savings account in 1998 its call centre was overwhelmed and executives were called in to help open a tsunami of cheques-in-the-mail.

Nevertheless, at the height of the dot.com boom, I left to join the board of Earthport.com, the person-to-person payments provider. We raised £25m in March 2000, just in time to see the 'dot.com bubble' burst. By mid-2001, decision-making in the tech world had slowed to a crawl and budgets were slashed and I left Earthport to get married and regroup. In what was perhaps an eerie portent of the financial crisis, I then spent two years as the legal and compliance director for GE's first mortgage business – which has since come in handy.

But the internet world soon re-heated. In the summer of 2004, I joined a team of disenchanted Egg execs and other finance refugees, who were trying to figure out how to launch 'eBay for money', soon to become Zopa. Our leader, Richard Duvall, was convinced we were in the grip of what he called "the individual revolution". He believed that the internet was enabling 'free-formers', or self-directed individuals, to seize control of their lives. They'd begun responding to what others were buying on eBay and Amazon. They had 'unbundled' music albums and holiday packages to create their own, using Napster and Expedia. They'd used Kelkoo, the retail price comparison site, for 'tactical shopping'. Richard and the Egg strategy team – James Alexander and

Dave Nicholson – believed that financial services would be next. A bunch of us helped prove that by launching Zopa's person-to-person lending platform in March 2005. Zopa members' activity now occupies more than 1% of the UK's personal loan market. In March 2008, I began consulting to Amazon.com on its plans for an e-money offering in Europe, and I've continued specialising in online retail financial services ever since.

The writing began in October 2004, when I felt emboldened to observe that:

> "The 'Can Do' mantra of corporate culture has been replaced by the 'Why Can't I...' of consumer culture".[3]

As Negroponte had urged back in 1996, the digital era *had* transcended 'gadgets'. The focus had shifted to "what people actually do that is slow and inconvenient, and which technology could readily improve, rather than the technology itself." The new language was about *activities* that consumers controlled, rather than gadgets or web sites themselves: 'online auctions', 'music downloads', 'comparison shopping' and 'home shopping'. In that article, I warned that "Businesses have to be ready to do, sell or make stuff the way each customer wants it to be."[4] In 2006, I even suggested that legislators were beginning to require offline businesses to implement the benefits of successful online business models. I called that process 'Counter-regulation'.[5] But given its roots in the rules and architecture of participative 'Web 2.0' services, I could have called it 'FolkLaw'.

After some early posts on Zopa's blog, I decided to start my own in November 2007. I chose 'Pragmatist' as the title because it seemed to reflect the 'test and learn' process by which digital entrepreneurs have been facilitating consumers' quest for control. The title also gave me enough scope to record my observations outside the legal and financial services space.

When choosing the posts for this first book in the Pragmatist series, it struck me how the same themes that emerged during the initial 'credit crunch' of 2007-2008 remain with us – Indeed, the consequences of massive borrowing, waste and over-expenditure will not leave us for at least the rest of the decade.

This financial, economic, political and social crisis may have its roots in the dark days of US sub-prime lending. But, as this collection of posts demonstrates, we cannot only blame a zealous belief in the efficiency of markets, the 'Greenspan put' and Gordon Brown's 'Golden Rule' of public sector borrowing. Greed and stupidity are rife in our markets, political and regulatory corridors and living rooms throughout the world. We need to engage in more 'intelligent practice' if we are to make any sustainable improvements to our financial system.

This book addresses that challenge in five chapters. In the first, we consider the rise of pragmatism out of a bottom-up desire to know what 'works' in the midst of widespread disillusionment with society's institutions. In the second chapter, we look at the difference between 'institutions', which exist largely to solve their own problems, and 'facilitators', which exist largely to solve their customers' problems. In the third, we focus on the economic environment in which our financial system operates, including the prevalence of greed and stupidity and a dearth of scepticism and critical thought. In the fourth chapter we look at how financial services are evolving in the context described in the previous three chapters. Finally, we see how financial regulation that was ironically intended to protect us actually works to our detriment, and what changes could be made to encourage the growth of simple, low cost – and useful – financial services that move money efficiently to where it's needed.

---

1   *Economic Possibilities for our Grandchildren*, 1930
2   Negroponte, N., *Being Digital*, Coronet Books, 1996
3   "Why Can't I...?" is the New "Can Do", *Computers and Law*, October/November 2004.
4   See also: Seybold, P., Marshak, RT & Lewis, JM, *The Customer Revolution*, Random House Business Books, 2002.
5   Counter-regulation, *Computers and Law*, April/May 2006

CHAPTER 1

RISE OF THE PRAGMATISTS

Why Pragmatist?

A pragmatist is someone who acts in an informed way to control his or her personal environment, using a combination of theory and practice. Or as John Dewey would have it, a practitioner of "intelligent practice versus uninformed, stupid practice".[6] I chose 'Pragmatist' as the name for my blog, because, as a lawyer working on innovative solutions to consumer problems, I see plenty of examples of both types of practitioner and wish to encourage everyone to become one of the former.

A pragmatist does not slavishly follow rules, or political dogma, or 'positive thinking' or 'the herd'. To do so would assume a world that is somehow ordered, whereas almost all significant events in history are Black Swans[7] – surprise events that have a huge impact and which we rationalise by hindsight. Rules and dogma can turn out to be badly wrong. The herd is eventually caught out. So it is dangerous to blindly follow, and we must minimise our exposure to the downside of surprise events, yet maximise our exposure to the upside.

The combination of theory and practice that qualifies as 'intelligent practice' involves trial and failure. It involves being sceptical and 'contrarian'. It encompasses the aggressive tinkering of entrepreneurs – 'facilitators' – who have helped us wrest control of our own life experiences from the one-size-fits-all experience offered by 'institutions' – the established music labels, book publishers, retailers, package holiday operators, banks and political parties. We consider the finer points of difference between facilitators and institutions in Chapter 2. But for current purposes let's just say that facilitators exist to solve their customers' problems, while institutions exist to solve their own problems at their customers' expense.

Facilitators make the difference between us 'raging against the machine' in a lone, fragmented way and acting together as individuals in a highly concentrated fashion. And the giant, boundary-less online community of practising individuals and facilitators characterises the 'architecture of participation' that lies at the heart of 'Web 2.0'.[8]

It is tempting to infer causality here. But it's safer merely to observe that the rise of Web 2.0 has coincided with declining levels of trust in our institutions.[9] For instance, it has been found that:

> "the level of alienation felt towards politicians, the main political parties and the key institutions of the political system is extremely high and widespread [yet...] very large numbers of citizens are engaged in community and charity work outside of politics. There is also clear evidence that involvement in pressure politics – such as signing petitions, supporting consumer boycotts, joining campaign groups – has been growing significantly for many years."[10]

In other words, it may be that institutions are being marginalised by people pragmatically engaging with each other in their own digital communities, not only for retail purposes but also political, environmental, health, and economic reasons.[11]

Big questions arise.

Could today's successful facilitators become tomorrow's institutions? Are today's institutions somehow doomed? Or can they become facilitators by realigning with the activities of individual citizens and consumers?

Inverting the institutional narrative

The problem with modern institutional narratives is they ignore the elephant in the room – you. Individuals are ultimately responsible for each wave of service provider overtaking the last.

You decide what to pay and to whom, and whether to pay at all. The real challenge for institutions is an internal one about how to regain their relevance to *you*. As we explore further in Chapter 2, they've lost sight of their role in solving consumers' problems in favour of solving their own. They've ceased to be – and ceased to be rewarded as – facilitators. And unless they can regain their role as facilitators of people's actual and desired activities, they will die the lingering death of the spurned institution.

Yet the institutional narrative dominates our society, even though faith in our institutions has plunged over the past few decades, and we have turned to direct action and single-issue campaigns as an alternative to formal politics. Former footballer Eric Cantona has provided an example of how those narratives clash:

Hey Eric, lend your Euros directly to other people

Like previous financial crises, this one won't end until individual and collective confidence in banks and the financial system is restored.[12] And while it's all very well for the Eurozone's political masters to be demonstrating their 'political will' to hold the Eurozone together at individual taxpayers' expense, their attempts at restoring confidence have not exactly impressed Southern Europe's debtors...

The implications of the one-size-fits-all Eurozone monetary policy also seem to be regarded as just as unfair by German taxpayers[13] and the French savers supporting Eric Cantona's suggestion for mass bank-withdrawals last December[14] as by those hitting the streets of Greece and Ireland. The *Guardian* quoted Valérie Ohannesian, of the French Banking Federation, as saying Cantona's appeal is "stupid in every sense". Yet, crucially, she did not explain *why* people should feel confident about leaving their money on deposit, or why it is fair that banks receive taxpayer bail-outs while taxes increase and spending is cut. In the absence of any other explanation, each bail-out undermines our confidence even further, to the point where we hit the streets and seriously consider Cantona's suggestion. Politicians need to listen to this bottom-up narrative if they are to properly understand our motives at the ballot box (or in favouring the rise of email over posted letters, or internet shopping over some high street retailers, or Google over News Corp) and where those motives may lead.

Eric Cantona's confident call for mass withdrawals hints at the fact that people are prepared to put their money where their mouth is. But it would be futile for those with surplus cash languishing in low-interest savings accounts to withdraw it all and hide it under their beds. Instead, they should join those who already put their money to work helping others, by lending it directly on peer-to-peer lending platforms to creditworthy people and businesses at a decent rate that also represents a decent return. Indeed, in response to the imposition of a debit card fee by some US banks, activists campaigned for a 'National Transfer Day' that resulted in credit unions receiving $4.5bn in new deposits and 650,000 new customers.[15]

Innovation doesn't 'kill' anything

As someone who's been involved at one bleeding edge or other of retail innovation for over a decade, I flinch when anyone mentions the words 'critical mass'.

Innovation is hard because it always means change. And change is a difficult process – more so for most of the population than the comparative minority of innovators and early adopters who preach it. So, while it's vital that there are evangelists for change who are passionate and completely biased in their view of the benefits of the new and the disadvantages of the old, it's also important to temper their message when addressing the wider world. After all, new products don't need to 'kill' old ones, they need to co-exist, at least in the short to medium term.

Tempering the discussion of innovation is more easily said than done. Once upon a time, change was only whispered at the top of organisations or society, and you or me would get fired or killed for daring to speak its name. The joyous challenge presented by social media is that discussions about change are open to everyone.

For instance, I've been directly involved in e-payments for over a decade, and various people have called for 'the death' of cash or cheques at one point or another. Some still do. But, while this resonates with the faithful innovators and early adopters, it is neither helpful to most people's acceptance of innovative financial services nor to the process of getting those services released. Laggards seize upon the moral panic about the 'death' of something held dear as the reason not to embrace change, often relying on 'hard data' from the current process against merely honest estimates of the benefits to be gained from implementing the new one. And that can be enough to eliminate virtually any innovative project from a crowded institutional boardroom agenda. The announcement of the 'abolition' of cheques awakened deep resistance, and provided the laggards with a platform from which they can make change harder than it needs to be.[16]

But innovation doesn't have to be positioned that way. I can readily see why cash (or cheques) are still a vital payment option in certain scenarios, and the challenge for facilitators is to create an alternative that is genuinely more useful. In the meantime, the various payment methods should co-exist, and if people naturally refrain from taking up new ones, or gradually abandon one form or another until it becomes untenable, so be it.

The weakness of positive thinking

As an avowed pragmatist, I savoured Barbara Ehrenreich's 'Smile or Die', about the tyranny of positive thinking – the idea that positive thoughts alone can achieve an outcome.[17]

Barbara traces the rise of 'positive thinking' out of the misery of Calvinist soul-searching, through 'christian science' to popular psychology and self-help books, to academic psychology and, finally, to major corporations, banks and other institutions. The cult of positive thinking tends to result in the ritual sacrifice of critical thinkers for having a 'negative attitude'.

Barbara patiently explains why positive thinking will not of itself produce a desired outcome, and how it has proved positively harmful to suppress critical thought and to avoid addressing genuine doubt and 'negative' sentiment. She points out that 'positive' does not equate to 'good', and 'negative' does not equate to 'bad'. After all 'bad' stuff happens to 'good' people too.

Of course it is helpful to approach life positively. Merely committing to a particular goal is enormously helpful – if not critical – to achieving it:

> "Until one is committed, there is hesitancy, the chance to draw back, always ineffectiveness. Concerning all acts of initiative (and creation), there is one elementary truth the ignorance of which kills countless ideas and splendid plans: that the moment one definitely commits oneself, then providence moves too. A whole stream of events issues from the decision, raising in one's favour all manner of unforeseen incidents, meetings and material assistance, which no man could have dreamt would have come his way. I learned a deep respect for one of Goethe's couplets:
>
> 'Whatever you can do or dream you can, begin it.
> Boldness has genius, power and magic in it!'"[18]

But as the Scots soon learned, commitment is not determinative of the outcome.

It is common among athletes to imagine or envisage a successful performance in a given scenario to improve their confidence when the time for performance arrives. That should *help* their performance. But it's only one contributing factor rather than the 'cause' of any success.

If positive thinking alone were enough to guarantee success, everyone would be successful, and North Korean leader Kim Jong-il really would be able to control the weather with his mood.[19]

Instead, we must struggle on, doing our best to figure out and cope with all the variables likely to significantly affect a scenario, including all the bad things that might happen. The fact that the world is heavily influenced by surprise events, or Black Swans, means we can only minimise our exposure to the downside and maximise our exposure to the upside. Approaching that *process* proactively and positively is clearly going to be helpful but, again, it won't of itself be determinative of success.

Ultimately, Barbara questions the effect of positive thinking on 'happiness'. Here, it's easy to see that strict adherence to positive thinking – and the corresponding suppression and repression of all 'negative' news, thoughts and emotions – does not end well. Barbara cites the Lehman Brothers top brass, Dick Fuld and Joe Gregory, who may have made plenty of money eschewing analysis and 'going with their guts', but eventually blew the bank. We'll meet more of these sorts of characters in Chapters 3 and 4. Joe Stalin, too, was big on 'optimism' and a little hard on 'defeatist' critics and others who didn't 'get with the programme'. And doubtless Kim Jong-il constantly curses the naysayers for the under-performance of his 'optimistic' regime and the shitty weather.

And let's not forget, among the long list of victims, all the angry and confused positive-thinkers out there who hot-desked, travelled incessantly, ignored their friends and family, slept with their Blackberries and generally drank the corporate Kool-Aid, only to discover they were surplus to requirements.

I hope they don't get fooled again.

Gen Y: rise of the pragmatists

I attended the launch of 'The Faith of Generation Y'[20], which the *Daily Telegraph* responded to on its front page.[21]

In the course of the co-authors' presentation of some key findings, one of many interesting observations struck me in particular. Bob Mayo explained that Generation Y[22] people are not so reactive to organised religion as Generation X,[23] who tended to have had religion forced on them as kids. Instead, Gen Y'ers are just as interested to hear what religion is and what it stands for, as any of the other spiritual messages out there. But they aren't interested in whether the message represents the 'truth' in some dogmatic sense. They want to know, pragmatically, whether it 'works'.

So you will find a Gen Y person chilling out in a church because it is a chilled, spiritual place to be, rather than because he 'believes'.

Interestingly, Bob says this attitude is actually *fostered* by Gen X people. As parents (and teachers, I presume), Gen X'ers tend to be friends with their kids and/or tolerant or permissive of independence, critical thought and discussion, rather than authoritarian or controlling as their own parents' generation tended to be.

I suspect this observation may explain two drivers in the decline to low levels of trust in our institutions. First, Gen X'ers may be reacting to the tendency of previous generations to trust in or tolerate institutions, regardless of how poorly they deliver on their objectives and obligations (although such institutions were smaller and Victorian charitable activity much more prevalent than today). Second, while Gen Y'ers may be free of the emotionally reactive element of Gen X's attitude to institutions, they are very focused simply on how those perform, and respond accordingly.

So if you thought the internet and Web 2.0 marked a revolution in personalisation, you ain't seen nothin' yet.

Snake oil and the 'science' of liberty

On 1 December 2010, I happened across the following Tweet:

> "http://bit.ly/gMGro6 expect to hear a lot more about Oxytocin in marketing writings going forward. This is a good piece."

The link took me to a paper called 'The Science of Liberty' by Paul Zak, self-styled "founder in the field of neuroeconomics".[24] It purports to provide a basis for lighter financial regulation and was funded partly by the John Templeton Foundation, a conservative philanthropic organisation, whose president also supports Let Freedom Ring (the lobbying outfit which also supports the right wing Republican Tea Party movement in the US) and partly by the Gruter Institute for Law and Behavioural Research.[25]

I hope I don't do Paul's reasoning any injustice, but I understand his thesis to be as follows:

- "[A] brain chemical called oxytocin (ox-ee-TOE-sin) is released when a stranger takes money from his or her pocket and intentionally gives it to another person in order to demonstrate trust tangibly... the more money the person receiving the trust-denoting transfer receives, the more his or her brain releases oxytocin. Oxytocin levels, in turn, predict how much the second person will reciprocate the first person; that his, how trustworthy she or he will be." This process is "nearly impossible to inhibit".

- However, 2% of those studied did not reciprocate, and "[T]here is a technical word in my lab for these folks: bastards. Not people you want to have a coffee with... On the other hand, two percent isn't bad. It means most people most of the time are trustworthy, and the others can be identified with a slight bit of investigation."

- Participants go out of their way to punish moral violations in the market "when observers of ethical violations are in a position to punish the violators".

- As a result of these findings, Paul asserts, "virtue is in fact the very foundation of trade... The market can be fabulously large if most people, most of the time, behave morally, and if their moral tendencies are supported by a legal system in which property rights are protected and contracts enforced."

- Accordingly, Paul asserts, "Economic systems that provide for freedom and limited oversight recognise human dignity and the desire for self-direction." Such "economies are complex, adaptive, and evolving systems that need no controller. Just a clear set of rules that are enforced by some independent regulatory body."

- "A number of studies have shown that too much oversight crowds out our innate sense of virtue (Gneezy and Rustichini, 2000). A fine for every violation decouples transgressions from the moral violations to a 'greed is good' justification. This is Enron and the like" [a reference that includes Ford (exploding Pinto gas tanks) and the USSR].

• In other words, the Enron scandal was created by overly intrusive regulation, and therefore we should have less of it.

Ironically, far from presenting a basis for lighter financial regulation, I'm afraid Paul Zak's research into the effects of Oxytocin shows exactly why people need greater protection from the snake oil salesmen, who understand its effects only too well.

We don't need research into Oxytocin to tell us that 'bread and circuses' and 'porkbarrelling' buys votes, or that bribes buy re-zoning and so on. The "bastards" *are* out there. And even if their presence were empirically measured to be two percent of the population, that would mean there were actually a heck of a lot of them and they can do a lot of damage.

None of this stacks up in any event. Without compelling everyone to submit to an Oxytocin release test, it often takes more than "a slight bit of investigation" to identify 'bastards'. And their "ethical violations" can be similarly tough to uncover and publicise (as we shall see in Chapter 5). Further, the observers are frequently not in any "position to punish the violators". Nor do we have an adequate or "clear set of rules that are enforced by some independent regulatory body", as we shall also see in Chapter 5.

This renders groundless the assertion that "virtue is the very foundation of trade". As observed in 'Animal Spirits: How Human Psychology Drives the Economy, and Why It Matters for Global Capitalism':

> "...[T]he unvarnished invisible hand story, although right in a fundamental way, is wrong at the level of detail and approximation that is necessary to explain what we need to know about macroeconomics.
>
> The old story about capitalism is correct: it gives us what we think we want. But capitalism does not act as its own policeman if we fail to watch over it and give it proper directions. It actively, competitively, seeks the most profit-maximising

opportunities. Capitalism will follow such opportunities wherever they lead us...

If [we] are willing to pay for real medicine, it will produce real medicine. But if [we] are also willing to pay for snake oil, it will produce snake oil. Indeed, nineteenth century America had a whole industry devoted to fraudulent patent medicine."[26]

Finally, and perhaps most notably, Alan Greenspan, former chairman of the US Federal Reserve advocated light touch financial regulation for 40 years, and has lived to regret it:

"In Congressional testimony on October 23, 2008, Greenspan acknowledged that he was 'partially' wrong in opposing regulation and stated 'Those of us who have looked to the self-interest of lending institutions to protect shareholder's equity – myself especially – are in a state of shocked disbelief.' Referring to his free-market ideology, Greenspan said: 'I have found a flaw. I don't know how significant or permanent it is. But I have been very distressed by that fact.'

Rep. Henry Waxman (D-CA) then pressed him to clarify his words. 'In other words, you found that your view of the world, your ideology, was not right, it was not working,' Waxman said.

'Absolutely, precisely,' Greenspan replied. 'You know, that's precisely the reason I was shocked, because I have been going for 40 years or more with very considerable evidence that it was working exceptionally well.'

Greenspan admitted fault in opposing regulation of derivatives and acknowledged that financial institutions didn't protect shareholders and investments as well as he expected."[27]

Now, I'm no fan of the Nanny State. I don't believe regulation acts as a market catalyst. And I've written often in support of better regulation rather than simply more of it. It's also clear that the financial regulation failed to avert the latest financial crisis, and on its own is unlikely to avert the next. But it would not be wise to reduce the amount of financial oversight. In fact, more sunlight and transparency – not less – is critical, and regulation does have a role to play in achieving those outcomes.

Our defences against disaster weaken over time

In August, a month before Occupy Wall Street launched,[28] there was an interesting post at Zero Hedge speculating on the core theme behind the meltdowns of the recent past:

> "The bottom line is that if we continue to let the top 1% – who are never satisfied, but always want more, more, more – run the show without challenge from the other 99% of people in the world, we will have more Fukushimas, more Gulf oil spills and more financial meltdowns."[29]

Danger lurks in positioning only the "top 1%" as greedy or lacking in critical thought or the tendency to "challenge".

Surely not all people in the top 1%, socioeconomically speaking, fail to think critically or act responsibly. Idiots in positions of influence or command would be powerless without yes-men and flunkies ready to act without question, who genuinely and honestly believe it's their job to simply do what they're told, no matter how weird it seems.

It seems clear from the devastating impact of recent natural and man-made disasters, that our defences to key threats seem to weaken steadily over time, regardless of the adequacy of the initial defensive position. We can see that process at work not only in our poor defences against financial mayhem but also in, say, the state of the New Orleans flood defences or the failed attempts to implement tsunami alert systems ahead of the Boxing Day Tsunami of 2004.

It's easy to blame cost-cutting itself, and management greed or short-term shareholder expectations as its source. Or perhaps even a general human tendency towards complacency. It's easy because such 'causes' let 99% of us off the hook.

But surely that's the root cause of the problem. We *all* know that our society's defences to major threats weaken over time, but we lay the blame on a select few – e.g. Zak's 2% who are "bastards" or Zero Hedge's "top 1%" – instead of each bearing the responsibility to constantly question the readiness of those defences, whether as head of state, chief executive, directors, auditors, lawyers, staff, parents, investors, taxpayers or voters. We must not cast ourselves – nor allow ourselves to be cast – as powerless victims.

Yet, as I hope this book shows, we *are* beginning to question our defences against disaster, to challenge our institutions by promoting facilitators, their empowerment of individuals and all the ensuing bottom-up changes these have wrought.

Fool's gold, fool's paradise

Gillian Tett's 'Fool's Gold',[30] is an insightful, frank and highly readable account of the credit crunch.

It explains the unfolding disaster from the standpoint of the JP Morgan staff who unleashed the Bistro-style CDS derivative into an environment of such stunning irrational exuberance, greed, negligence, recklessness and downright fraud that it left even the creators aghast.

Importantly, Tett's narrative tellingly confirms a string of cultural problems that we're told again and again abound in the capital markets trading 'pit': regulators whose remit and resources prevent them seeing the financial world holistically, a commission/bonus-driven sales mentality that often ignores the limits of the hallowed Gaussian 'models', banking 'groups' that disguise dysfunctional silos, the cosy social contract banks enjoy with government. It's little wonder that everyone lost sight of the big picture – and that our faith in these institutions has been utterly shattered.

And it ain't over yet.

Amidst all the talk and shuffling of deckchairs little is actually being done to avoid or minimise exposure to Black Swan events. Hedge funds have scrambled to avoid the sunlight,[31] like the 'swaps' world did previously, and the quest for transparency has degenerated into protectionist farce. Competing government and opposition plans for the financial sector[32] ensured regulatory paralysis when structural and cultural reform would have been most achievable.

As a result, we're still living in a fool's paradise.

Does occupation work?

Much is being written about Occupy Wall Street and similar expressions of mass dissatisfaction about our financial system. In particular, many are giving advice on more practical alternatives to occupation,[33] which misses the point:

> "Occupy Wall Street is [a] leaderless resistance movement with people of many colours, genders and political persuasions. The one thing we all have in common is that We Are The 99% that will no longer tolerate the greed and corruption of the 1%. We are using the revolutionary Arab Spring tactic to achieve our ends and encourage the use of non-violence to maximise the safety of all participants."[34]

In other words, occupation is what people do when their faith in all the immediately practical alternatives is exhausted.

But why? Does mass occupation 'work'? I mean, is Egypt now a better place? Wouldn't it be better to withdraw completely and assume the foetal position under your duvet?

While I don't believe these protests have any *causal* connection with the changes that are democratising the financial markets, they are critical insofar as they represent a peak in our society's dissatisfaction with its institutions. I mean, the occupations are not intended to shock people or wake them up, like a strike or a noisy protest march outside Parliament. Quite the reverse: pitching your tent in the beating heart of a giant city is a sign of utter confidence that every rushing passer-by, every person who reads the paper or watches the evening news will understand exactly why you're there.

For this reason, such occupations are a sign that the majority of us have rounded the change curve. It means we've moved beyond 'shock' at how broken things are, through 'denial' and beyond 'anger and blame' – even though that appears to be what all the signs are about. Those people wouldn't be there if they did not instinctively sense that *we would all understand* why. That we all share the sense that something has to be done. The reason they're gathering is to figure out *what* is to be done.

Ironically enough, these occupations mean we're moving on.

6   http://en.wikipedia.org/wiki/Pragmatism
7   http://en.wikipedia.org/wiki/Black_swan_theory
8   http://oreilly.com/web2/archive/what-is-web-20.html
9   http://ec.europa.eu/public_opinion/archives/eb_arch_en.htm; A Eurobarometer poll has also found that only "50% of EU citizens trust their local and regional authorities, a level slightly higher than for the European Union (47%). This level of trust in the local and regional authorities is considerably higher than the level of trust in national governments or parliaments (34%)" http://ec.europa.eu/public_opinion/archives/ebs/ebs_307_en.pdf
10 http://news.bbc.co.uk/1/hi/uk_politics/4753876.stm
11 http://www.makeitanissue.org.uk/2007/01/power_commission_archive.php#more; http://www.dothegreenthing.com/; http://www.cancerresearchuk.org/; http://www.oxfam.org/en/
12 G. Akerlof and R. Shilling, *Animal Spirits: How Human Psychology Drives the Economy, and Why It Matters for Global Capitalism*, Princeton University Press, 2010
13 http://www.bbc.co.uk/news/world-europe-11768732
14 http://www.guardian.co.uk/world/2010/nov/20/eric-cantona-bank-protest-campaign?CMP=twt_gu
15 http://en.wikipedia.org/wiki/Bank_Transfer_Day
16 The decision to phase out cheques is a classic example. Abolition of cheques sparked moral panic (http://news.bbc.co.uk/1/hi/business/8569895.stm) and an eventual U-turn (http://moneyfacts.co.uk/news/money/cheque-u-turn-haile-das-victory-for-common-sense130711/).
17 B Ehrenreich, *Smile or Die*, Granta Books 2010. It's also worth catching Jon Stewart's interview with Barbara on the Daily Show: http://www.thedailyshow.com/watch/wed-october-14-2009/barbara-ehrenreich.
18 W. H. Murray, *The Scottish Himalaya Expedition*, 1951.
19 http://en.wikipedia.org/wiki/Kim_Jong-il#cite_note-Pierre_Rigoulot_2005-87
20 Sylvia Collins-Mayo, Bob Mayo, Sally Nash, Christopher Cocksworth, *The Faith of Generation Y*, Church House Publishing, 2010
21 http://www.telegraph.co.uk/news/newstopics/religion/8042110/Young-people-have-faded-memory-of-Christianity-says-Church-book.html
22 http://en.wikipedia.org/wiki/Generation_Y
23 http://en.wikipedia.org/wiki/Generation_X
24 http://www.brightsightgroup.com/topics.asp?speaker=277
25 http://www.templeton.org/who-we-are/about-the-foundation/mission; http://www.thenation.com/article/god-science-and-philanthropy?page=full; http://www.teapartypatriots.org/; http://www.letfreedomringusa.com/; http://www.gruterinstitute.org/Home.html
26 G. Akerlof and R. Shilling, *op cit*
27 http://en.wikipedia.org/wiki/Alan_Greenspan
28 http://occupywallst.org/about/

29 http://www.zerohedge.com/article/japans-nuclear-meltdown-economic
    -meltdown-and-gulf-oil-meltdown-all-happened-same-reason?utm_
    source=feedburner&utm_medium=feed&utm_campaign=Feed%3A+zerohedge
    %2Ffeed+%28zero+hedge+-+on+a+long+enough+timeline%2C+the+survival+
    rate+for+everyone+drops+to+zero%29&utm_content=Netvibes
30 *Fool's Gold: How Unrestrained Greed Corrupted a Dream, Shattered Global Markets
    and Unleashed a Catastrophe*, Little, Brown, 2009
31 http://www.guardian.co.uk/business/2009/jul/21/hedge-funds-oppose-eu-regu-
    lation
32 http://www.independent.co.uk/news/business/news/tory-plan-to-scrap-fsa-in-
    banking-shakeup-1753588.html
33 http://blogmaverick.com/2011/10/14/my-soapbox-advice-to-the-ows-move-
    ment-and-then-some/
34 http://occupywallst.org/

CHAPTER 2

FACILITATORS VS INSTITUTIONS

Brand as facilitator, not institution

I was jamming with former ad-man turned marketing exec, Mark Nepstad, one Saturday about the role of brands and their agencies in social media (as you tend to do on Shiraz) when he showed me a graphic from David Armano's excellent 'Logic and Emotion' blog, depicting the multiple 'Influence Ripples' of conversations about a product in various social media, as if a pebble had been dropped into each pond.[35]

What struck me was how this would give a supplier an 'aerial' view of their consumers' community, enabling the supplier to better organise itself to facilitate its customers' experience.

As I've suggested above, it is the 'architecture of participation' created by various Web 2.0 facilitators that has been a very real catalyst in this rise in personal, informal, direct action. It has enabled millions of us to experience what it's like to personalise the one-size-fits-all consumer experiences offered by the likes of music labels, book publishers, retailers, package holiday operators, banks and political parties. So it can be said that the facilitators of this architecture are making the difference between us 'raging against the machine' in a lonc, fragmented way and acting together as individuals in a concerted fashion. And that's a thrilling ride.

Used to facilitate rather than dictate customers' activities, the data about a supplier's 'influence ripples' amounts to yet another tool with which a brand, as facilitator, can strengthen the architecture of participation and further assist consumers to personalise their experiences involving the brand's products – a 'virtuous circle'. Conversely, the very nature of the architecture in which the influence is rippling means that any supplier who is perceived to be using, or likely to use the data for Orwellian purposes – to manipulate or interfere for its own institutional ends, rather than its customers' interests – must find itself in a 'vicious circle' of adverse comment. There are numerous instances of this dynamic at work in the privacy sphere,[36] as well as fall-out from Ryanair's spat with an 'idiot blogger', for example.[37]

Reassuringly, I see that Mr Armano came to a similar conclusion in his own post, entitled (coincidentally, I swear) 'Brand as Facilitator', with some more very nice graphics.[38]

Of love marks and the institutionally deluded

In his book 'Convergence Culture',[39] Henry Jenkins discusses the attempts to transform brands into 'love marks' by developing more intense relationships with consumers.

The implicit assumption of 'big brands' seems to be that mere interaction can create these relationships. Yet, as Henry points out in the context of gaming communities, the brands' own product terms and behaviour are arguably more important. The point is whether the increased interaction between the 'brand' owner and consumers facilitates the resolution of real consumer problems, or improves consumers' day-to-day activities in some compelling way. But marketing strategies usually seem to view the world through the products the provider has chosen to sell, rather than from the standpoint of what the individual consumer might need to buy. And that implies the business ultimately exists to solve its own problems rather than those of its customers. In which case, the business is exposed to the downside of the trend towards increasing consumer power over the design and supply of the products they use or consume.

As a case in point, I had a conversation earlier this year with a payment industry executive who believes that the most important brand that is present during a consumer's purchase from a retailer is the brand on the consumer's debit or credit card. This of course ignores the fact that the consumer's activity in question is 'buying' a widget of the right quality from a merchant they trust, rather than merely 'paying' for it. I suggested to the payments exec that, if he was right, the brands of the card schemes and issuers should top all the 'trusted brands' surveys. After looking at two such surveys,[40] he agreed that consumers think their retailers are doing more for them than their banks or card schemes.

The Long Tail: define 'head' and 'tail'

Early on, I was struck by a fascinating post by Chris Anderson responding to *Harvard Business Review* analysis of sales patterns in the music and home-video industries to see if they support or undermine the idea that Long Tail theory distinguishes e-commerce from bricks-and-mortar retailing.[41]

HBR had suggested that the 'blockbuster theory' holds even for e-commerce. So online businesses should also focus their resources on promoting hit products rather than a long list of obscure products each of which may only suit a small band of consumers:

> "A balanced picture emerges of the impact of online chan-
> nels on market demand: Hit products remain dominant, even
> among consumers who venture deep into the tail. Hit prod-
> ucts are also liked better than obscure products. It is a myth
> that obscure books, films, and songs are treasured. What
> consumers buy in internet channels is much the same as what
> they have always bought."

As ever, we need to be careful about definitions. Chris Anderson points out that:

> "'Head' is the selection available in the largest bricks-and-
> mortar retailer in the market (that would be Wal-Mart in this
> case). 'Tail' is everything else, most of which is only available
> online, where there is unlimited shelf space."

So 'hit' products don't necessarily equate to the 'Head', nor 'obscure products' the 'Tail'. Using Chris's definition, the *HBR* data supported more 'tail heavy' consumer demand on the sites analysed.

We see this definitional problem in relation to financial services market analysis, and it frames two distinctly different challenges – one that banks seem to embrace, and the other taken up by new facilitators.

In a very helpful post on 'The Long Tail of Banking', Chris Skinner wrote [my emphasis]:

> "The *Long Tail in banking would be a mass market of niche microgroups* that incur no cost overheads to manage but, for each transaction, creates a small profit... You want to reach people who were previously underserved, because it would not be profitable....We are talking about children, students, the unbanked, the underbanked, the grey market, the welfare market, the pensioners, the migrant workers and more. And we are talking about social lending and saving, [e-payments]... we need to look at prepaid and mobile for these folks."[42]

I don't disagree with Skinner's call to action. But I understand him to be defining 'head' and 'tail' in terms of customer types rather than product selection – current bank customers are the head and "niche microgroups" are the tail. Accordingly, Chris's long tail challenge is how to deliver *existing* bank products to the tail, which assumes those products are useful to those people.

However, I share Chris Anderson's view of the head and the tail in terms of the breadth of *product selection* (and related customer need), not the customers themselves. Seen in these terms, the long tail opportunity is to use online platforms to offer a broad enough or sufficiently flexible range of financial services to enable every customer to find or create the experience that is right for him or her personally.

To turn this around, it seems Web 2.0 is now disrupting traditional retail banking because banks have followed a traditional 'blockbuster' approach – marketing comparatively few, very inflexible products (which represent the 'head') and relying on those to attract most of the market, rather than trying to market the 'long tail' of products that would solve every person's individual savings, investment, borrowing and payments needs. Online facilitators, like Zopa, have spotted this, and created the means to enable consumers to create, or find and buy, the financial product that is right for each of them personally, in the same way that they can now design their own holiday instead of taking a package holiday, or buy individual music tracks instead of albums. Using these facilitators, consumers effectively create thousands or even millions of their own 'products'.

Currently, financial regulation, tax subsidies and the resulting liquidity constraints limit a feasible long tail strategy to markets for personal and small and medium-sized enterprise (SME) loans. But the right reforms would enable people to finance each other's mortgages, mutually assure general insurance, offer short-term trade finance for SMEs and so on, *depending on their individual product need.*

I take Chris Skinner's point about mobile being critical to reaching 'niche microgroups' of customers, but designing all 'long tail' products for a single access technology will constrain utility and product take-up. To facilitate the long tail effect, product access has to be as porous as the participants need it to be in order to create their own 'product' whenever and wherever is convenient or useful for them. For example, you should be able to share or publish your loan request or 'listing' via your PC or mobile to all the social network platforms, in the same way you can share a blog post that you like. It's about maximising flexibility and utility rather than constraining it. Think e-money itself, rather than the medium used for its storage or transfer.

The blockbuster approach has led financial institutions to treat, say, 'payment' as an activity bounded solely by their limited service capability. In-store payments aside, it has been a real struggle to enable individuals to make payments and money transfers when and where they want to. Yet, from a customer standpoint, the act of payment is always embedded in a much longer 'marketplace' process. Lack of support from banks has left retailers and 'shopping cart' providers or 'aggregators' to develop most of the tools that support that process flow. Integrating payments with online shopping carts and ordering pipelines to create a satisfactory customer experience occupied the first 10 years of e-commerce development, and many still get it wrong. There have been many false starts in the mobile payments space (not to be confused with mobile banking), and services in that segment still suffer from a lack of standards, portability and interoperability. This makes it tough to enable each user to make up his or her own payment solution to suit a specific scenario. But efforts by Amazon, Google and others are suddenly bearing fruit.

Mobile banking, on the other hand, still suffers from the old blockbuster thinking – merely offering access via your mobile device to the same old, inflexible bank products, rather than enabling users to make up their own. I'm sure the long hand of the Web 2.0 trend will enable this eventually. But I doubt that a bank will be the facilitator.

Long tail financial services: passion and connection

There have been plenty of interesting insights emerge from debate about the long tail. One of those was Kevin Kelly's_build on Seth Godin's discussion of the "three profit pockets" on the tail of product popularity.

In brief, Seth says that the first two – at or near the head – are profitable for the creator, while the third – the long tail – is only profitable for the aggregator:

> "The most common misconception about Long Tail thinking is that if you don't succeed at pocket 1, don't worry, because the tail will take care of your product and you'll just end up in #2. That's not true. #2 isn't a consolation prize for mass market losers. Mass market losers are still losers. In order to become a mass market star you make choices about features and pricing and quality – and if you lose that game, there's no reason to believe that those choices are going to pay off for a different market."[43]

Kevin (with whom Chris Anderson agrees) says you shouldn't conflate the views of creator and aggregator, but view each section consistently from each perspective. That way you see clearly the challenge that each faces when products are in the long tail – albeit one that aggregators are able to meet more easily:

> "...if we view the long tail as a market of a different type, as a market of enthusiasm and connection, then as the long tail

expands, this increases the chance of two enthusiasts meeting, and so the longer the tail, the better. The first two pockets of the curve are trying to maximise profits; the last pocket of the long tail is trying to maximise passion and connectivity.

There is one further indirect advantage to the long tail. Since your creation now exists in a market (where it would not have existed at all before) it can, if you are lucky, start to migrate uptail."

This emphasises why creating a social network among interested buyers and sellers of each of the products, or sets of products in the long tail, becomes critical to maximising revenue from it:

"A social network is a social structure made of nodes (which are generally individuals or organisations) that are *tied by one or more specific types of interdependency*, such as values, visions, ideas, financial exchange, friendship, kinship, dislike, conflict or trade."[44]

Facilitators' discussion boards, blogs and social network services all clearly help enable those buyers and sellers to find their type of interdependency – so do open marketplaces like online auctions, or simply knowing what people who bought one item also bought, or what other profiles they viewed, and so on. But ultimately, transparent, reliable, timely pricing and product description are key to sales.

Applying this to retail financial services is interesting, given the heat generated by current economic and market conditions.

Where's the 'passion'?

The last time the most people got the most passionate about retail financial services was in the early '90s when many houses prices plunged into negative equity (the dotcom bubble-burst affected far fewer consumers.

The Internet wasn't around commercially to help people get out of negative equity in the early '90s, but a whole 'specialist' (and substantially sub-prime) mortgage industry ignited around the fact that 25% of the people who'd had a mortgage from a high street institution suddenly couldn't get one. More recently, Northern Wreck sent a shock wave rippling through the UK population, and similar disasters struck at US retail borrowing sentiment. Occupy Wall Street and similar movements demonstrate how widespread this shockwaves have travelled.

Where's the 'connectivity'?

In the early 1990s, connectivity arose because lawyers and other advisers knew which of their clients who were 'battlers' and worth a punt. They arranged loans from other clients or themselves, starting new mortgage and loan providers and brokerages in the process. All manner of strange, alternative finance deals became available – a veritable long tail of mortgages, secured and unsecured loans. Daytime television advertising hasn't been the same since.

Today, when the banks are on their knees, the Internet and social network services are there to facilitate connectivity amongst the passionate and social lending facilitators[45] are also enabling individual consumers to lend and borrow at rates that suit them personally. Rigid tax and regulatory requirements are inhibiting the development of a long tail of products, but further shocks and ensuing passion is likely to bring the required reforms.

Mystics and revolutionaries – the drivers of innovation

You'll have gathered by now that I'm fairly sceptical when it comes to messages from our institutions, and I support positively disruptive innovation and innovators whenever possible.

Bob Mayo, of St Stephen's church in Shepherd's Bush,[46] is an innovator in one of the most conservative institutions on the planet, so I'm always fascinated to read his crisp observations in 'Parish the Thought', Bob's weekly 200-word email. In one of those emails, Bob hit on a theme at the heart of Web 2.0:

> "The gospel passage for this Sunday sees Jesus feeding 5,000 hungry people with five loaves and two fishes (Matthew 14:13-21). Making the world a better place is not something limited to Jesus 2,000 years ago. Helping the poor and hungry and looking after those who are vulnerable or in need is the responsibility of us all. Nouwen (1994) says that we need to be 'mystics' and 'revolutionaries'. The 'mystic' is concerned

with changing the human heart and the 'revolutionary' is concerned with changing human society. In case you think of yourself as being one or the other, Nouwen also says that every real 'revolutionary' is challenged to be a 'mystic' at heart. 'Mysticism' and 'revolution' are two aspects of the same desire to make the world a better place to live. *The whole socio-political world in which we live is geared against change.* This should mean that we do not want to try. William Wordsworth talked about being as 'impatient as the Wind'." [My italics.]

Two particular aspects chime with the disruptive trends associated with 'Web 2.0'. First, there is the overall point that successful disruptive business models are motivated by making the world a better place to live for individual people, personally. It's not about institutions, it's about improving each individual customer's personal experience through an 'architecture of participation'.

The second aspect is the idea that "the whole socio-political world in which we live is geared against change". One cause of our declining faith in our institutions is perhaps the realisation that regulations and rules (including the business rules by which institutions and big suppliers choose to transact with us) have tended to be written to suit the way institutions wish to do things, rather than what might suit us personally. We are told that these regulations and rules are hard to change, but become cynical when we see Parliament rush through laws that curb civil liberties or regulators move quickly to protect the banks but were slow to act in case of consumer detriment, or big corporations get tax bills magically waived or show they *can* immediately cease an activity after years of stonewalling.

Such inertia is why it takes 'shocks' and a lot of energy from people who are "as impatient as the Wind" to kick us all the way along the 'change curve' to the point where we plan to do things in a different way.

It would also seem that the notion of the long tail as "a market of enthusiasm and connection" where people find niche products that suit them personally chimes with the idea that we need 'mystics' and 'revolutionaries' to make the world a better place.

'Platforms' as 'markets'?

A hat-tip to The Bankwatch for pointing out Umair Haque's interesting post 'What Apple Knows That Facebook Doesn't'.[47]

I understand Umair to be saying that Apple has adopted a 'market' business strategy, whereas Facebook is taking a 'platform' approach. Apple facilitates an increase in flexibility and utility for its customers, while Facebook channels its users into functionality of its choosing and exposes them to advertising. Apple will dominate, Facebook is somehow doomed.

But how does this improve on O'Reilly's explanation that the success of Web 2.0 businesses stems from their 'architecture of participation'? He sees the internet as a 'platform' but with a different set of rules for success. So it seems we should see platforms as a *feature* of markets or certain market phases, rather than "platforms as markets", as Umair would have it.

And you could easily switch Umair's examples to show that Facebook and Apple actually have a lot in common

Facebook has actually made the Internet and internet technology more usable for people who want to network, socially or otherwise. Yes, there are some crappy apps (just as in Apple's world), but angels and venture capitalists are funding the expanded development of some apps that have acquired significant numbers of users overnight – hence the notion of the Facebook economy. It may be hype, to some extent, but what investor-fest isn't? The basis of competition has changed, because you can launch a business today with a tenth of the funding you needed seven years ago. The domino effect might be seen in the way incumbents are effectively forced to market themselves in the social network services space.

Apple, on the other hand, sought to make each of the iPod, the iPhone and now the iPad the dominant platform in its space. Apple drip-feeds new functionality, new versions and content deals with the majors as a way of trapping people on those platforms. The result is a standards war between device manufacturers and operating systems, which is frustrating for anyone who wants truly interoperable mobile applications and music that will play on any device.

As a result, the approaches of Facebook and Apple may actually be more similar than different. Each has created an architecture of participation, and time will tell which is more successful at sustaining it, but there's scope for them both to 'win'.

Are you dealing with introverts or extroverts?

A survey on Mashable suggested that most social networkers are in fact introverts.[48] That means they are driven by their own thoughts and feelings, whereas extroverts – at the other end of the continuum – are driven by external interaction.

For any online service provider this begs the question whether your customers are introverts, extroverts or in the middle, and how you should manage your marketing and communications for each type. However, assuming your objective is to generate passion and connection amongst your customers as a community, then perhaps it's better to view your staff and customers as a team comprising all types who need to get along.

Furthermore, as Idea has pointed out, the introvert/extrovert dichotomy is but one aspect of personality and how personalities interact in a team scenario:

> "In the Myers-Briggs assessment, personality characteristics are categorised along four continuums: Introvert/Extrovert; Sensing/Intuition; Thinking/Feeling; and Judging/Perceiving.
>
> ...
>
> Whereas introverted team members need extroverts to initiate spontaneous verbal discussions, extroverts value an introvert's capability for problem solving based on careful reflection and consideration of all ideas.
>
> ...
>
> intuitive members need sensing personalities to remind them of facts and limitations. Conversely, sensing individuals need intuitive members to remind them to think outside of the box.
>
> ...

As team members, thinkers are effective in articulating logical reasons behind decisions, while feelers can bring people together.

...

A team needs the right mix of judging and perceiving personalities to ensure adaptability as well as adherence to project boundaries and deadlines."[49]

Now I don't want to reach any conclusions for all you introverts, but some takeaways might be:

1 An extrovert staffer could be asked to initiate discussions and debates, but might need to take some care to leave the discussion and conclusion open to engage the introverts;

2 Provide opportunities for people to think outside the box;

3 Articulate not only the *reasons* for decisions but also acknowledge how the decisions make people *feel*; and

4 Demonstrate flexibility, but *set expectations about any constraints on flexibility*, like resources and deadlines.

Turning complaints into fixes, features and products

Ever since GE required me to get my Six Sigma[50] green belt, I've been convinced that complaints can have a significant positive effect on costs and revenues. But only when you're prepared to painstakingly work from identifying the critical expressions of dissatisfaction to implementing the fix, feature and maybe even the product, that solves the problem.

That isn't to say every business problem can't be solved without an enterprise-wide investment in Six Sigma, LEAN or some other problem-solving methodology.

Simply implementing a process for accurately classifying customers' initial expression of dissatisfaction *from the customer's standpoint* will get you going along the right path. It's then pretty much common sense to identify the most common issues, figure out their scale or value, and spend a proportionate amount in resources to find their root cause, the best fix for the money and a trigger that tells you if and when the problem resurfaces.

This is not a 'customer service' issue. It's the very essence of a business.

Allowing all functions to see and contribute to the complaint resolution process will ensure that bad stuff doesn't get hidden. You can then throw blame out the window and take a holistic, realistic view of significant problems and the resources available to put them right for good.

Enable your best customers to create financial services

All vendors and platform operators feel an obligation to look after their best customers. But to what extent are those customers really allowed to influence product development?

In the course of researching a presentation on the long tail of payments services for GikIII[51] (a two-day workshop on the inter-sections between law, technology and popular culture), I was struck by how the following observations combine:

- There is value in marketing 'long tail' products if adding selection is cheap: Anderson;
- Compared with heavy users of online retail services, light users much prefer better selling products; both prefer 'hit' products more than those in the tail; *but it is the heavy users who venture into the tail*: Elberse;[52]
- Successful Web 2.0 businesses are those that facilitate an 'architecture of participation': O'Reilly;
- "Lead-user product development can be a far more effective means of innovation than conventional prod-uct development in a closed system": Sheahan (citing von Hippel) and giving various illustrations of the same concept in Threadless, Jones Soda, LEGO's Mindstorms Users Panel and Linux.[53]

Suggestions that even 'excellent retailers' have run out of ways to improve the online shopping experience, and the only scope for real innovation is on the buy-side, are way overdone.[54] Improved tools for buyers as well as 'power sellers', are an important set of features in the overall consumer experience mix. And revealing to light users the products bought by prolific buyers might move those products up the 'tail'.

Sadly, however, research by Datamonitor suggests financial institutions are too mired in last century's anxieties to let their online customers loose with a bunch of web-based tools.[55]

Of living the iLife, dinosaurs and data portability

I'm not here to sound the death knell for Apple, but the announcement of the iCloud is a defining moment in the company's development. Will Apple remain a facilitator, or become an institution that exists only to ensure its own survival?

The 'cloud' or utility model for computing is not new. Consumers in particular have held their data and basic applications 'in the cloud' ever since adopting public email services, blogging services and so on. What's new about the iCloud is the automated way in which all a consumer's different types of content may be synchronised and otherwise 'managed' across all the consumer's (Apple) devices.

The centralised omnipotence this may hand to Apple seems an attempt to reverse a 20-year trend toward enabling consumers to control their own data. In this sense, the iCloud appears to be the sort of product a major bank or telco 'dinosaur' would introduce in a last-ditch effort to survive by locking-in its customers. Facilitating data portability is absolutely critical (along with personal data protection and security), if the iCloud is to be seen as a consumer 'enabler' rather than a predatory move by an ageing institution.

But consumers consider data portability to be important? I mean, I'd like to think that Apple's early, tech-savvy customer base would realise it's a bad idea to hold all your applications and data with a single provider, just as financially savvy folk realise the benefit of a fully-diversified investment portfolio. I have an iPhone, an iPad and an iTunes account; but I also have a Dell laptop and a Dell PC. Those computers run Microsoft's Windows and Office package, and I have a Hotmail address; but I very deliberately browse with Firefox; blog via Blogger; Tweet; hang out on Facebook and follow various blogs using Netvibes. I use Spotify, not iTunes, as my main music service. In other words, I'm not going to let any one provider see, process, hold or control all my data – or even have a complete back-up or copy. To me, that would feel closed and controlling, rather than enabling.

But, ironically, I suspect many people in the mainstream would look at my system diversity and see it as a hassle or a problem to be solved by a single service provider. Which is why Apple may be quite genuinely facilitative in its vision for the iCloud, rather than a dinosaur that's spotted a meal. In that case, educating consumers about the value of diversification in technology as well as financial services seems important.

The cheetah generation: will facilitators grow faster in Africa?

Recent problems in the Eurozone have heightened the need to find new markets. So perhaps it's a great time to recognise the step-change in technology adoption that's occurred amongst sub-Saharan Africa's 'cheetah generation'.[56]

'Africa' obviously represents a vast array of very different peoples and 'socio-economies', as Hans Rosling brilliantly illustrated at TED.[57] As at 2006, that included a communications divide:

> "Egypt had 11 times the fixed line penetration of Nigeria. While sub-Saharan Africa (excluding South Africa), had an average teledensity of one percent, North Africa (Algeria, Egypt, Mauritania, Morocco, Tunisia) had a comparable average of eleven percent. Almost three-quarters of the continent's fixed lines were found in just six of the continent's 55 countries."

Enter the mobile phone. From a mere 0.2 subscribers per 100 inhabitants in 1996, take-up rocketed in the next 10 years to 21.6 subscribers per 100 inhabitants, while the number of fixed line subscribers rose from 1.9 to 3.2 per 100 inhabitants in the same period.[58]

> "By the end of 2011, the entire continent of Africa will be connected to no fewer than nine undersea broadband cable initiatives. Africa will have access to over 17 terabytes of designed broadband capacity. If mainframes and punchcards served as the innovation catapult for Silicon Valley's cheetah generation, then connectivity is poised to be Africa's innovation catalyst. Since mobiles first went mainstream in Africa at the turn of the century, mobile penetration has exploded to approximately 450 million subscribers...
>
> Africa's growing list of technology hubs are the cheetah generation's digital proving grounds. Appfrica Labs opened its doors in Uganda in 2008. Since then, three additional tech hubs have opened around the continent. Limbe Labs Ventures Cameroon and Banta Labs in Senegal launched in 2009. Nairobi now has its very own centre of excellence in the iHub innovation centre...
>
> Keep a very close eye on Africa's young population, that 450m number growing up with a mobile phone in their back pocket."[59]

The explosive growth of M-Pesa, the successful person-to-person mobile payment system[60] also suggests that Africans may be more willing to rapidly embrace disruptive finance models than Westerners. Perhaps this is partly because they've been more poorly served by banking and telecommunications to date. But is the Kenyan architecture of participation also stronger than ours? For instance, do African communities share a greater sense of personal trust than in the West? Why is it that adoption of M-Pesa's functionality explodes in Africa while UK consumer groups celebrate the decision not to abandon the cheque as a "victory for common sense"?[61]

At any rate, it seems the trend toward the growth of facilitators at the expense of institutions is set to grow fast in sub-Saharan Africa, at least where that can occur via mobile networks.

Steampunk mobile

The arrival of mass personal digital communications in previously remote areas might teach us a lot about enabling people everywhere to gain greater control of their lives – particularly as those scenarios have remained free of the top-down institutional constraints imposed by many of our retail brands to solve their own problems rather than ours.

You don't need to be literate or even numerate in the true sense to communicate in the mobile world. For example, mobile numbers have become personal identifiers for many in India.[62] And even the more literate among us need help in deciphering symbols used by young people when text messaging. So, while basic mobile phone-based literacy and learning programmes are themselves important, they shouldn't distract us from the potential for mobile phones to enable people to seize control of their lives in circumstances where they have been 'left behind' by government and other institutions.

The rapid adoption of M-Pesa is a case in point. And the technology hubs used by Africa's 'cheetah generation' are also worth watching carefully. In addition, gaming applications have been effective in educating Indian children and improving their social mobility where charity and government social programmes have failed:

> "The use of educational games on the mobile phones facilitated new ties between participants across gender, caste and village boundaries, and the new social relationships that developed transferred to real world, non-gaming settings."[63]

Design firm Adaptive Path has also studied the mobile phone usability and design needs of people in rural India. Those people cited the following features and functionality as the most important to them:

- Calling;
- Texting (using voice to text or with assistance);
- Music;
- Camera;*
- Microphone;

- Speaker;
- Airtime;
- Battery Level.

* While most research participants did not have mobile phones with cameras, this was cited as a desired feature.[64]

Saving contact information was the single most challenging task for non-literate users to perform. So they don't bother, preferring to scroll through call logs to numbers they recognise (the personal identifiers I mentioned earlier).

To remove the complexity of entering and saving data, vizualisers Adaptive Design borrowed from industrial tracking processes to suggest enabling users to photograph a QR Code or 'MobilGlyph' that contains the unique data required to populate a phone's contacts database. Of course, the process of producing accurate and reliable MobilGlyphs would also need to be efficiently administered.

But Adaptive Design's approach to the challenge of handset design is even more intriguing. They found "there is a strong culture of reselling, re-purposing, cobbling,[65] and repair throughout India and this is especially true in rural villages". So Adaptive Design turned to Steampunk which, they explain, "...reflects the design and craftsmanship of the Victorian era" and echoes the 'architecture of participation' at the heart of Web 2.0:

> "Similar to the exposed inner workings of a motorcycle, works of art created to reflect the Steampunk genre possess a look of craftsmanship and cobbling. It's an aesthetic that invites the touch of the human hand and it encourages engagement and fosters curiosity and play.
>
> Taking cues from Steampunk's 'hack-able' aesthetic, we made the phone look like an object that can be opened and tinkered with by exaggerating seams and making the mechanisms to open the device obvious... vibrant sound is an important part of Indian culture and ... We chose to emphasise these elements by giving them a larger portion of the phone's physical real estate ... Gauges are commonly used to convey quantitative information on cars and motorcycles in

rural India. We echoed these familiar interface elements to communicate battery level and airtime minutes. Finally, we drastically reduced the feature set of the phone, allowing us to assign each function a single button. We borrowed 'stop' and 'start' buttons from stereos and placed them on the side of the device. Taking cues from a radio dial, our Steampunk phone contains a scroll wheel – creating a strong and intuitive relationship between the physical interface element, the gesture, and the UI inside the screen."

It seems to me that this design makes the device simple and usable without dumbing it down. As Adaptive Design point out:

"Empathic design is not about forcing conventions and models on users that feel foreign, it's about empowering users with technology that feels appropriate and familiar. Designers and user experience professionals have a responsibility to avoid viewing illiteracy as a deficiency, but as an important design consideration for a large portion of the world."

It seems that empathic design and has a big future globally, and the evolution of software and technology in India and Africa have a lot to teach us about how to meet our own consumer challenges.

---

35   http://darmano.typepad.com/logic_emotion/2008/01/influence-rippl.html [hard to replicate in our format].

36   http://en.wikipedia.org/wiki/Online_privacy#Privacy_within_social_networking_sites

37   http://www.theregister.co.uk/2009/02/25/idiot_blogger/

38   http://darmano.typepad.com/logic_emotion/2008/07/brand-as-facila.html

39   H. Jenkins, *Convergence Culture: Where Old and New Media Collide*, NYU Press, 2008

40   http://www.utalkmarketing.com/Pages/Article.aspx?ArticleID=16879; http://www.moreaboutadvertising.com/2010/10/marks-spencer-rivals-top-list-trusted-brands/

41   http://www.longtail.com/the_long_tail/2008/06/excellent-hbr-p.html; http://harvardbusinessonline.hbsp.harvard.edu/hbsp/hbr/articles/article.jsp?ml_action=get-article&articleID=R0807H&ml_issueId=BR0807&ml_subscriber=true&pageNumber=1&_requestid=29909

42   http://www.thefinanser.co.uk/2008/07/the-long-tail-o.html

43   http://www.longtail.com/the_long_tail/2008/07/kevin-kelly-the.html

44   http://en.wikipedia.org/wiki/Social_network_analysis

45   http://en.wikipedia.org/wiki/Social_lending

46 http://www.ststephensw12.org/
47 http://thebankwatch.com/2008/08/23/platform-vs-market-logic-applied-to-p2p-lending/;
    http://blogs.hbr.org/haque/2008/08/what_apple_knows_that_facebook.html?cm_mmc=npv-_-WEEKLY_HOTLIST-_-AUGUST_2008-_-HOT-LIST0822
48 http://mashable.com/2008/08/15/irony-alert-social-media-introverts/
49 http://www.idea.org/personality.html
50 http://en.wikipedia.org/wiki/Six_Sigma
51 http://www.law.ed.ac.uk/ahrc/gikii/2008.asp
52 http://blogs.hbr.org/cs/2008/07/the_long_tail_debate_a_respons.html
53 http://www.amazon.co.uk/Flip-Succeed-Turning-Everything-Know/dp/0007275986/ref=sr_1_1?ie=UTF8&s=books&qid=1221142648&sr=1-1
54 http://thebankwatch.com/2008/09/11/retailers-have-improved-the-online-shopping-experience-as-far-as-they-can/
55 http://www.finextra.com/fullstory.asp?id=18963
56 http://www.ghanacybergroup.com/articles/getart.asp?id=370&MC=ART&cat=5
57 http://sdj-pragmatist.blogspot.com/2009/10/human-development-index-is-personal.html
58 http://www.itu.int/ITU-D/ict/statistics/ict/index.html; http://www.itu.int/ITUD/ict/statistics/ict/graphs/af1.jpg
59 http://www.theglobeandmail.com/news/technology/africas-booming-techspace-will-define-the-continents-future/article1563090/
60 http://en.wikipedia.org/wiki/M-Pesa
61 http://moneyfacts.co.uk/news/money/cheque-u-turn-hailed-as-victory-forcommon-sense130711/
62 http://www.economist.com/blogs/babbage/2010/05/mobile_phones_and_identity
63 http://siteresources.worldbank.org/EDUCATION/Resources/278200-1121703274255/BBL_4_12_2010_Mobile_Phones_Kam1.pdf
64 http://www.adaptivepath.com/blog/2009/05/18/steampunk-a-mobile-device-concept-for-rural-india/
65 By which I understand them to mean 'cobbling together', rather than making shoes!

CHAPTER 3

THE ECONOMY: GREED AND STUPIDITY ARE WINNING

What is more socially important than the creation of wealth?

I'VE READ article after article, and book after book about our financial crisis, and the really bad news is not the poor risk management and regulatory failings, nor banks' ram-raids on the Treasury to cover their losses while paying giant bonuses, nor the £81bn in public sector spending cuts, higher unemployment and lower house prices, nor a decade of economic malaise.

The really bad news is that the root cause of the crisis is that we have no higher, universally accepted social ambition(s) than the accumulation of wealth, so we're doomed to repeat the whole sorry saga.[66] In 1930, John Maynard Keynes, the great god of economic thought, wistfully looked forward to a new world without greed and acquisitiveness:

> "When the accumulation of wealth is no longer of high social importance, there will be great changes in the code of morals. We shall be able to rid ourselves of many of the pseudo-moral principles which have hag-ridden us for two hundred years, by which we have exalted some of the most distasteful of human qualities into the position of the highest virtues."[67]

So when *will* the accumulation of wealth cease to be of high social importance?

When there is enough wealth? Surely not. There will never be 'enough wealth', because we seem to have no idea what 'enough' is as a society, nor how to figure that out.[68] There will always be greedy people, and people in great need, who will be compelled to find a way to accumulate wealth. Especially when the financial crisis is putting everyone under pressure to make a penny to survive. So I doubt we'll change people's desire to accumulate wealth, although, as we'll see in this chapter, their acquisitiveness may be dampened by 'conspicuous thrift' and a focus on sustainable capitalism.

If we are going reverse an ugly trend in our financial system we must agree on at least one higher ambition than the accumulation of wealth.

What's it to be? Learning? Charity?

When asked for his advice to bankers recently, Lord Rothschild simply responded: "Behave well. Give back more."[69]

Greed is still good

I'm troubled by whether audiences believe the ending to the movie Money Never Sleeps is a positive 'Hollywood' resolution, rather than a grimly ironic testament to persistent greed.

Long story short, while Gordon Gecko (immortalised by the line "Greed...is good") has just done time for crimes committed during Wall Street, it turns out he'd syphoned $100m into a Swiss account in his daughter's name. Her 'liberal' plan had been to give it to charity. But, with a little encouragement from Gordon, her fiancé convinces her to 'invest' it with him and her old Dad in a 'clean-tech' alternative energy company. Gordon then diverts the cash, betraying the couple's trust and dashing their financial and nuptial plans. His suddenly pregnant daughter never wants to see Gordon again, and certainly doesn't want him to anywhere near his grandchild ... In the final scene, however, Gordon is redeemed – and heals the emotional rift between the unhappy couple – when he drops by to announce that he's deposited a freshly laundered $100m in the bank account of said clean-tech energy company.

Cue wedding and dancing.

I guess one can't blame a daughter for wanting her dear old dad to be around her child, even if he is only anxious to teach the kid the equivalent of safe-cracking. But I was struck by the fact that she's also billed as a 'liberal' and that she and her fiancé share a passion for alternative energy. Their easy forgiveness of her reptilian father suggests that the Bernie Madoffs of this world – indeed our financial institutions – can redeem themselves simply by investing their ill-gotten gains in 'worthy causes' rather than by behaving ethically from the outset.

In other words: greed is still good. The end justifies the means.

If Hollywood had been confident that our values had changed, the young lovers would have been united in their strenuous execution of a citizens' arrest.

This is not 'just a movie'. US authorities are resigned to the theme:

> "Speaking close to the two-year anniversary of Lehman Brothers' collapse, Mr [Hank] Paulson [former Treasury Secretary] said that while he welcomed much of the new financial regulation, it would not be enough to prevent another crisis. 'We have to assume that regulation won't be perfect. We'll have another financial crisis sometime in the next 10 years because we always do.'"[70]

And timely that UBS, the global investment bank, should announce that it won't be pursuing the former senior managers who appear to have put in place "incentives...to generate revenues without taking appropriate consideration of the risks [that]...facilitated losses" because any such court action would be "more than uncertain", expensive and "lead to negative international publicity and thus hamper UBS's efforts to restore its *good name in the markets*" [my emphasis].[71]

What's that a 'good name' *for*, exactly?

The nature of scepticism

What struck me most after reading 'The Big Short'[72] and 'Fooling Some of the People All of the Time'[73] is the dearth of critical thought in the financial community. So imagine the thrill I experienced on seeing the Financial Reporting Council's 'Feedback Paper' entitled '*Auditor Scepticism: Raising the Bar*'.[74]

This paper confesses that auditors aren't really sure what the word 'scepticism' means:

> "While responses to the Discussion Paper demonstrate widespread agreement on the critical importance of auditor scepticism to audit quality, there is less agreement on the nature of scepticism and its role in the audit."

Well, when the judges are stuck for the ordinary meaning of a word, they head for the Oxford English Dictionary. It defines a 'sceptic' as "a person inclined to question or doubt accepted opinions." So, I'm thinking the nature of scepticism might be... the inclination to question or doubt accepted opinions.

But rather than handing out dictionaries, the FRC has decided to undertake work in the following areas:

- Ensuring that there is a consistent understanding of the nature of professional scepticism and its role in the conduct of an audit.
- Reviewing ISAS (UK and I) for possible ambiguities in relation to the nature and importance of professional scepticism, and proposing such changes as may be needed to make sure the position is clear.
- Reviewing ISQC (UK and I) 1 to ensure that it has sufficient requirements and guidance relating to the need for firms to have appropriate policies and procedures for promoting the competencies that underlie professional scepticism.
- Considering how the application of scepticism can be made more transparent.
- Considering, with other parts of the FRC, whether there is a need for guidance on the approach to be taken by auditors when considering the presentation in the financial statements of matters that have been the subject of significant challenge by the auditors.

In other words, so dire are the standards in the audit world that *they have to teach professionally qualified auditors how to be sceptical.*

It's as if we had to train our senior detectives not to believe everything suspects tell them.

You couldn't make this up.

Analyse this

Auditors, and others interested in the nature of scepticism (feel the irony) will have enjoyed the *FT's* coverage of stock market analysts' reluctance to write 'sell' notes on the companies they cover.[75]

In theory, the distribution of sell, hold and buy ratings should be equal. Yet Bloomberg found that 60% of analysts' ratings are 'buy'. And 'buy/hold' ratings together outnumber 'sell' notes by 9 to 1.

One chief of US equity strategy was brave enough to be quoted as saying, "There is clearly a lack of willingness of management to deal with analysts who are highly critical."

McKinsey, the management consultancy, has also found that analysts are "typically overoptimistic, slow to revise their forecasts to reflect new economic conditions, and prone to making increasingly inaccurate forecasts when economic growth declined."[76]

Why do investors put up with this?

It should be self-defeating to obviously exclude or limit critical analysts' participation in briefings – either a sell signal in itself, or at least a signal that everyone should start asking a lot more questions. But ultimately the research highlights the fact that, for all the law on disclosure and directors duties, the stock market is dominated by salespeople.

Buyers beware!

Madoff victims should not blame the SEC

Something caught my eye in the *FT's* coverage of the SEC's inspector-general's report into the SEC's handling of the Madoff saga [my italics]:

> "Jacob Frenkel, an attorney with Shulman Rogers, said the report indicated that some SEC staff, 'failed to recognise a blazing fire because they were too focused on the

smouldering match in their fingertips.... Madoff investors would have been better off and *far more sceptical* had the SEC never investigated or conducted examinations.'"[77]

While the SEC has a lot of improvements to make, Frenkel's claim just doesn't stack up. Worse, blaming the SEC will mean that Madoff's victims will continue to behave in the way that got them into trouble in the first place.

In my book, victims really only have themselves and Madoff himself to blame, on three counts.

First, the substance of the complaints to the SEC only reflected what was being published by the likes of Michael Ocrant from 2001, and Harry Markopolos said it took him four hours to spot the Ponzi scheme in 2000, using publicly available documents.[78] And according to the *Telegraph*, Goldman Sachs also banned its asset management and brokering divisions from dealing with Madoff's funds 10 years ago, while "a raft of blue-chip financial institutions have suspected something was wrong for years."[79] So there's no reason that Madoff's victims and their advisers should not have detected these concerns with even a little scepticism.

Second, it's obvious from numerous official announcements that it often takes several years for the SEC's enforcement machine to engage and eventually produce a settlement or prosecution. And, of course, such proceedings are subject to the usual vagaries of the appeals process. While this is hugely frustrating for investors and competitors alike, it is clearly impossible to draw any conclusion from the fact that the SEC may be investigating some activity, other than that they are probably late to the scene.

Finally, what really seemed to cause Madoff's victims to invest was the bandwagon effect created by Madoff's skilful recruitment of socialites and other high-profile names as key investors. This meant that investing with Madoff was more of a social badge than a financial decision. And that is hardly something that the SEC can be expected to do much about.

The Age of Conspicuous Thrift

When the ladies of West London 'discovered' TK Maxx, the bargain fashion store, some years ago, it was almost a guilty secret.

While the odd bargain might have come from there, the latest designer dress or accessory was still purchased at more or less the full retail price in the West End, Knightsbridge or Kensington.

Since Christmas 2008, however, I've heard outright declarations that such-and-such an item was found at 'TKM' or its online rival, Asos, where sales over the 42 weeks to 16 January '09 rose by 108%.[80]

While the shift of clothing sales online is a remarkable enough trend in itself, given the Boo.com debacle, that's not why I've called it out. What's especially noteworthy is the open declaration of thrift by people who used not to wear it like a badge. Thrift has become conspicuous. A lifestyle choice, not an economic one. Economists have suggested that such a phenomenon would be termed the 'counter-Veblen effect' – i.e. "preferences for goods increase as their price falls, over and above the traditional supply and demand effect, due to a conspicuous thrift amongst some consumers."[81]

But we're not talking about the sort of conspicuous consumption passed off as thrift that might lead you to, say, "tear the roof off your home and replace it with solar panelling for $75,000 (£42,000), then boast about the cents you save on electricity."[82] 'Conspicuous thrift' seems to have a more pragmatic quality, and the explosion at Asos is consistent with the trends that have surfaced as 'Web 2.0'.

What does sustainable capitalism mean to you?

The term 'sustainable capitalism' encompasses many trends. John Ikerd's book deserves a mention, and Al Gore and David Blood use the term in a global, macroeconomic sense, backed by a sophisticated grass-roots programme.[83] However, a Google search reveals that debate over the meaning of the phrase is transcending the champagne and canapés at Davos – 'normal' people are really discussing and wrestling with the concept of living sustainably.

So what does sustainable capitalism mean to you?

Clues emerge from a number of converging trends:

- Politically, we still buy New Labour's twist on Thatcherite capitalism – it's okay for everyone to make money, so long as it's not at the expense of people on lower incomes. But we've now learned that this too can be overdone. Mightily. So, we're hastily adding the words "within reason" and trying to figure out what that really means. But we are far from entering a new age of conservatism, or attempting to maintain the status quo. We're in a hole, trying to dig our way out. And we are certainly not keen on the ugly notion of a 'no-growth economy'.[84] Nor should the desire to steady the financial system, by nationalising the banks if necessary, be seen as a vote for a centrally-planned economy or the mass redistribution of wealth from rich to poor. If anything, the rhetoric is for a return to consumerism in an effort to get people to at least buy *something*. But what? And for how much?

- As previously noted, this political process has coincided with a plunge in faith in society's institutions during the past 30 years, yet an *increase* in our political awareness and informal political action.

- Similarly, we've seen the rise of lean, IT-based platforms and marketplaces that have enabled us to wrest control of our own personal affairs from the one-size-fits-all experience offered by the likes of music labels, book publishers, retailers, package holiday operators, banks and political parties. Such facilitators are based on rules that promote openness, fairness, and transparency. As we'll see in the final chapter, these principles could extend to the democratisation of the financial markets, now that the individual taxpayer has a seat at the table. This is a bottom-up dynamic in which businesses need to facilitate, rather than dictate, to their customers.

- We've entered an Age of Conspicuous Thrift, as previously discussed, in which our preferences for certain goods will increase as their price falls, over and above the traditional supply and demand effect. This partly stems from financial necessity, but also from a social desire to appear savvy, pragmatic, authentic and environmentally aware. As opposed to Madoff investors.

- Of course, I would love to point to low cost government as a trend, but ministers and officials seem incapable of either preventing structural waste (initiating stupid projects) or improving operational efficiency. We've suffered from the same top-down thinking here, as we do in the financial services industry. Here, too, only bottom-up pressure from the participants will drive change – as it has done to some degree with MPs' expenses.

How all this looks and feels to you on a personal level is going to vary enormously. My own personal economic journey suggests that if you're in denial about any of these trends, you'll need a very different, pragmatic mindset to get comfortable in the new economy.

For me, that change in mindset evolved in stages from one of a fairly integrated cog in the corporate wheel in 1996, to thorough disillusionment in early 2004, to a fairly confident 'myself as a business' outlook from August 2005. Each of us is an entrepreneur, as Reid Hoffman has pointed out.[85] During that period, my own behaviour evolved from pressing my nose against the glass of Jaguar and Mercedes showrooms, to taking some satisfaction in the plan to drive a lesser marque until the wheels fall off. I still enjoy a decent glass of wine and the odd cigar, but I've also focused on the seven lifestyle aspects identified by Green Thing as helpful to the environment.[86]

As with most consumer choices, apparent inconsistencies from this perspective are actually driven by rational concerns from other standpoints. I won't be buying an electric sports car, because the core proposition is still 'speed', which feels too self-indulgent today. In fact, speed doesn't matter so much in a world where we work longer and harder, communication is instantaneous, and the UK roads are basically parking lots. Similarly, I ride to work on a motorcycle not because it goes fast, but because I can squeeze past all the parked cars, eliminate variation from the daily commute and use my time more efficiently. My 'green' electric sports car would just sit around in the traffic.

Zerozone? Short banks, long riot shields

In early 2010 we received the gory detail on the UK's financial vulnerability, including a barrage of charts from Zero Hedge that illustrated why the 'fasten seat belt' sign had been switched on.[87]

The charts showed the vast quantity of government debt issued by Portugal, Ireland (and/or Italy), Greece and Spain due to be repaid (or 'mature') simultaneously.

"So what?" you may have asked, if you'd been distracted by the UK elections.

The charts also revealed high scores in unemployment, budget deficits and public borrowing. So these countries will struggle to persuade investors to extend the due dates ('maturities') on existing loans – 'amend and extend'[88] – at affordable rates, if at all. And bail-out bodies like the International Monetary Fund will only help if the country concerned can implement 'austerity measures' to cut its deficit and get its economy under control.

The results of suddenly imposing such measures on citizens who hadn't realised how bad things were – or why – can be seen in the riots on Greek streets.

In fact, Zero Hedge tipped "the inevitable disintegration of the Eurozone and the upcoming eventual debt payment moratorium."[89] Which means there's a lot more mayhem to come for the European financial system. And even the ~~Euro~~Zerozone countries with the deepest pockets – like Germany and France – could need to rein-in substantially.

A good time to go long riot shields?

Does investment beat donations in sub-Saharan Africa?

While we're on the lookout for new markets to replace sagging Eurozone demand, reports in 2010 on why Asia took a knock due to problems in the Eurozone reveal that China will also be competing strongly elsewhere in order to reduce its reliance on

Europe.[90] The then research director at MF Global (as it then was) Nicholas Smith suggested:

> "China is significantly more exposed to Europe than the US... when the Euro plunged, one of the hardest-hit stock markets was China (because China now sells around a quarter more to Europe than to the US, and is highly sensitive to a slow-down in exports)."

So, for Asia, a weak Euro means:

> "Europe will buy less from Japanese companies.

> European companies, particularly German ones, will be made incomparably stronger and more competitive by the weak currency.

> Europe will buy less from China, which will damage Chinese growth and hence depress the prices of commodities, which 'anyway tend to follow a similar dynamic to the euro exchange rate.'"

One area of Chinese activity in the spotlight recently is sub-Saharan Africa. It's a sign of China's special focus on the region that 2006 was China's 'Year of Africa'. The web site devoted to Sino-African relations lists extensive contacts between the regions, and China recently announced its biggest deal in South Africa (to build a cement plant) since investing $5.5bn in Standard Bank in 2007.[91]

Western government hand-wringing about the ugly track record of some African nations seems to hide a reluctance to engage effectively in the region generally, as the blurb for Patrick Bond's book 'Looting Africa: The Economics of Exploitation' explains:

> "Despite the rhetoric, the people of sub-Saharan Africa are become poorer. From Tony Blair's Africa Commission, the G7 finance ministers' debt relief, the Live 8 concerts, the Make Poverty History campaign and the G8 Gleneagles promises, to the United Nations 2005 summit and the Hong Kong WTO meeting, Africa's gains have been mainly limited to public relations. The central problems remain exploitative debt and financial relationships with the North, phantom aid,

unfair trade, distorted investment and the continent's brain/ skills drain. Moreover, capitalism in most African countries has witnessed the emergence of excessively powerful ruling elites with incomes derived from financial-parasitical accumulation. Without overstressing the 'mistakes' of such elites, this book contextualises Africa's wealth outflow within a stagnant but volatile world economy."[92]

Other commentary on the significant development aid donors Germany, the UK and France is hardly flattering.[93] The US approach to the sub-Saharan region also needed realignment:

"With the collapse of the Soviet Union leaving both an economic and power vacuum, Bill Clinton began a programme of engagement with sub-Saharan Africa's economic powers like Nigeria and in encouraging passage the Congress of the Africa Growth and Opportunity Act which reduced trade barriers between the US and several African countries... George W. Bush followed on Clinton's achievements... and is widely regarded as the US President who did most for the advancement of the African people by bringing American money to bear on myriad social and health problems... [including] the goal of eliminating malaria and offering AIDS treatment to many who need it with the backing of $20bn in US aid grants."[94]

Against this background, it's worth carefully considering the criticism that:

"Chinese companies are the second-most likely (after India) to use payola abroad, according to Transparency International's Bribe Payers Index. Similarly, a World Bank survey of 68 countries last year found that the sub-Sahara leads in the 'percentage of firms expected to give gifts' to secure government contracts (43%). That meeting of the minds has made for hyper-efficient deal making in Africa."[95]

What does this really mean? Are 'bribe payers' to blame for ineffective donor programmes? Is the Bribe Payers Index really "improving the lives of millions" as is claimed? The criticisms of these league tables suggest they are not helpful in teaching us anything about the presence or effect of real corruption. In fact, Deborah Brautigam, author of 'Dragon's Gift: The Real Story of China in Africa' suggests the reality of Chinese investment in sub-Saharan Africa is rather more effective for the local people than Western aid programmes:[96]

> "As a donor, China's way has several advantages... The focus on turnkey infrastructure projects is far simpler and doesn't overstretch the weak capacity of many African governments faced with multiple meetings, quarterly reports, workshops, and so on. Their experts don't cost much. In addition, their emphasis on local ownership is genuine, even if it leads to projects like a new government office building, a sports stadium, or a conference centre. They understand something very fundamental about state-building – something that Pierre L'Enfant understood in 1791 when he teamed up with George Washington in newly independent America: new states need to build buildings and dignity, not simply strive to end poverty.

> The Chinese avoid local embezzlement and corruption by very rarely transferring any cash to African governments. There is almost no budget support, no adjustment or policy loans. Aid is disbursed directly to Chinese companies which do the projects. The resource-backed infrastructure loans work the same way.

> Of course those companies themselves might give kickbacks, as we've seen in Namibia..."

But that is not to say such alleged activity goes unchallenged, as reports of the Namibian case reveal. Nor does Brautigam gloss over China's role in the Sudan, which has attracted intense criticism. However, she points out:

> "First, China's role in Sudan has changed over the past several years. They were crucial in getting Khartoum to accept a joint UN/African Union peacekeeping force (one, by the way, authorised by the UN, but not funded as generously as originally pledged). They allowed al-Bashir's case to be sent to the International Criminal Court for prosecution for war crimes

(as Security Council members, they could have vetoed this). And as noted both by President Bush's special envoy, Andrew Natsios, and President Obama's special envoy, Scott Gration, Beijing is now working together with the US government and other major powers in developing joint strategies to bring the Sudanese government and the rebels to the negotiating table. As China-watcher Erica Downs put it, the West and China are now coordinating their 'good cop' and 'bad cop' roles in trying to end the crisis.

Second, there is no doubt that Beijing could have moved much sooner, and much more effectively, to become part of the solution. But they never held all the keys to solving the Darfur tragedy. In making a tactical decision to focus on China as the lynch-pin to solving Darfur's crisis, and using the 2008 Olympics as the pressure point, activists let the other major powers off the hook. To end the violence, Darfur needs a peace agreement, and that requires all the parties to participate in negotiations. The West has not yet been able to get all the major rebel groups to show up to start talking."

So, it's clear that Africa rewards investment in education and infrastructure, even if it comes in the form of work done by foreign companies directly rather than planeloads of cash. And it's also clear there is no substitute for effective international coordination to call recalcitrant regimes to account over human rights. That can't be achieved by a single nation – even a 'superpower', as we've seen from US military activity elsewhere.

Yet I wonder whether a bottom-up approach to investment in sub-Saharan Africa might also be far more effective than top-down donations? Apart from the provision of basic infrastructure and health services, supporting the rise of the cheetah generation and facilitators like M-Pesa and the technology hubs may do more to enable individuals to seize control of their own economic destiny than merely benevolent giving. Kiva, the microfinance provider, is a great example of this bottom-up approach:

"Kiva promotes:

- Dignity: Kiva encourages partnership relationships as opposed to benefactor relationships. Partnership relationships are characterised by mutual dignity and respect.

- Accountability: Loans encourage more accountability than donations where repayment is not expected.

- Transparency: The Kiva website is an open platform where communication can flow freely around the world.

  As of November 2009, Kiva has facilitated over $100m in loans."

This has parallels for the UK, to the extent that our government continues to rely on banks to lend more at a time when they are powerless to do so. Instead, the government should be flexing the tax and regulatory framework to encourage intermediaries that more efficiently connect those with surplus cash and those who need it.

Never retire

It will be fascinating to see if we get real transparency and competition in pension provision, now that the vast horde of public sector staff can no longer rely on the taxpayer to fund a nice, cosy retirement.[97]

No doubt the unions will fight for a reprieve, but ultimately public sector workers – like the rest of us – will have to focus very carefully on where their pension contributions go, and how much of their return is dissipated in fees, brokerage and dealing costs. *No one* will have the luxury of assuming they'll actually receive a pension (certainly not a life-sustaining one), just because they pay into one today...

The corporate pension deficit stands at £362bn, directly affecting 12m people.[98] And while all sorts of indexing and accounting tricks changes will be used to reduce the impact on company balance sheets, that won't translate into pension incomes for employees.

And there's no reason that the public sector will fare any better, absent the taxpayer safety net.

Strike all you like: the world has changed

I've never really understood the utility of modern labour strikes. And, given the timing of the current round in the UK, I suspect those who go on strike may not either. But I think the recent public sector strikes in the UK are a good sign.

It means the strikers and those who empathise (many private sector pensioners, for example) have moved on from the initial 'shock' of discovering there is no money to fund generous pensions.

And they have moved through 'denial' that this means *their own* pensions.

And they have reached the phase of 'fear and anger' about the fact that the world isn't as the same as they thought it was when they decided to do whatever job it is they've decided not to do while on strike.

We aren't talking about strikes arising from the mistreatment of a colleague, or any other point of principle. The current round of strikes is all about venting collective anger, though not quite in the Greek style. Yet. And anger on this scale – like the miners' strike in the mid-1980s[99] means the whole world has changed, not just your own lot.

Next stop: 'depression'. And then maybe 'acceptance', and a measure of 'understanding'. And, finally, 'planning' how to move forward into a very different future.

Cut Greece loose

Talk about capturing the *Zeitgeist* – there I was sitting in Porto in July 2011, reading about the Greek crisis in *The Economist*. The timing of my visit was good for the Portuguese, economically speaking (though our very generous hosts contributed most to the local GDP). In August, I made sure that Spain received some of the Pragmatic Pound. And I'd like to think I've been doing my bit for Ireland, albeit on the meter, by assisting a P2P financial services start-up there.

But I won't be bailing out Greece.

Tax-dodging, low productivity and overly generous pensions aside, *The Economist* reckons the key to that country's dismal plight is political patronage: "Greece needs transparent and impartial rules, but politicians are not keen to limit the scope for dishing out favours." Everything from railways to medical budgets leaks cash to powerful lobby groups, even though these bureaucratic emperors have no clothes.

In this sense the Greek rioters have more in common with the proponents of the 'Arab Spring' than their EU colleagues. As the ebbing economic tide exposes the littered wrecks of corrupt schemes and relationships, the have-nots are descending in droves on the survivors and their loot. In Syria, the crowds are putting the "squeeze on Assad" by demanding a 'civil democracy' that comprises free elections, freedom of speech and assembly, protection of minorities and an end to repression. The longer the government resists, the more citizens withhold their labour. Capital flees the country. In return, the regime dishes out more favours, stokes inflation and the country edges further toward meltdown. Egypt is clearly further along this curve. Libya further still.

Chaos is vital for renewal – though bloodshed is not essential. Back in June '09 I suggested that the UK's constitutional reform must be a messy process, and it's proving just that (though currently riot-free). A dynamic, open, democratic process that encourages broad engagement by all stakeholders cannot realistically be neat and linear.

But if the going gets really tough it's perhaps worth bearing in mind what Harry Lime says in the film of The Third Man:

> "In Italy for 30 years under the Borgias they had warfare, terror, murder, and bloodshed, but they produced Michelangelo, Leonardo da Vinci and the Renaissance. In Switzerland they had brotherly love, they had 500 years of democracy and peace, and what did that produce? The cuckoo clock."

Legend has it that Alexander the Great's decision to cut the Gordian knot with a sword-stroke resolved an intractable problem, pleased Zeus and earned him the kingdom of Asia.[100]

So cut Greece loose, I say. Only then will the Greeks have their next renaissance.

---

66 J. Lanchester, *Whoops!: Why everyone owes everyone and no one can pay*, Allen Lane, 2010
    http://www.nytimes.com/2009/04/03/opinion/03brooks.html

67 J.M. Keynes, 'Economic Possibilities for our Grandchildren', 1930.

68 I'm a fan of John C. Bogle's book 'Enough' [citation], though I struggle with his references to 'diamonds' which seem ironically materialistic to me.

69 Ian Hislop, 'When Bankers Were Good', BBC2, 2011: http://www.bbc.co.uk/mediacentre/proginfo/2011/47/ian-hislop-when-bankers-were-good.html

70 http://www.telegraph.co.uk/finance/financetopics/financialcrisis/8000696/US-risks-losing-superpower-status-unless-it-tackles-the-deficit-Henry-Paulson-warns.html

71 http://www.ft.com/cms/s/0/9bf5c07a-d766-11df-8582-00144feabdc0.html

72 M. Lewis, *The Big Short: Inside the Doomsday Machine*, Thorndike Press, 2010

73 D. Einhorn, *Fooling Some of the People All of the Time*, http://foolingsomepeople.com/main/

74 http://www.frc.org.uk/apb/press/pub2533.html

75 http://www.ft.com/cms/s/0/8d7529ec-53ed-11e0-8bd7-00144feab49a.html#axzz1HefKVLcJ

76 http://www.mckinseyquarterly.com/Corporate_Finance/Performance/Equity_analysts_Still_too_bullish_2565?gp=1, discussed here: http://www.simoleonsense.com/jonah-lehrer-optimism-bias-equity-analysts-still-too-bullish/

77 http://www.ft.com/cms/s/0/823958ba-97fa-11de-8d3d-00144feabdc0.html?ftcamp=rss&nclick_check=1

78 http://business.timesonline.co.uk/tol/business/industry_sectors/banking_and_finance/article5375374.ece

79 http://www.telegraph.co.uk/finance/financetopics/bernard-madoff/3868896/Bernard-Madoff-fraud-Increased-scrutiny-in-hedge-fund-industry.html

80 http://news.bbc.co.uk/1/hi/business/7837536.stm

81 http://en.wikipedia.org/wiki/Veblen_good

82 http://www.timesonline.co.uk/tol/comment/columnists/chris_ayres/article718421.ece

83 http://www.amazon.com/Sustainable-Capitalism-Matter-Common-Sense/dp/1565492064, http://online.wsj.com/article/SB122584367114799137.html

84 http://www.spectator.co.uk/business/the-magazine/magazine-lead-articles/3341791/why-theres-no-sense-in-no-growth.thtml

85 http://www.techcrunch.com/2009/03/05/read-hoffman-tells-charlie-rose-every-individual-is-now-an-entrepreneur/

86 http://www.dothegreenthing.com/

87 http://www.zerohedge.com/article/european-crisis-eight-simple-charts
88 Also 'extend and pretend' in more cynical market jargon. http://www.ft.com/cms/s/0/750b3140-8b61-11de-9f50-00144feabdc0.html?catid=93&SID=google
89 http://www.zerohedge.com/article/european-crisis-eight-simple-charts
90 http://ftalphaville.ft.com/blog/2010/05/11/226726/asia-takes-a-hard-look-at-europe/
91 http://www.focac.org/eng/zfgx/;
   http://blogs.telegraph.co.uk/news/alexsingleton/100002602/britains-aid-to-africa-is-a-disaster/
92 P Bond, *Looting Africa: The Economics of Exploitation*, Zed Books, 2006
93 http://www.neurope.eu/articles/74548.php;
   http://blogs.telegraph.co.uk/news/alexsingleton/100002602/britains-aid-to-africa-is-a-disaster/;
   http://africanpress.wordpress.com/2009/06/16/africa-french-aid-strategy-better-late-than-never-french-development-aid-will-target-agriculture-in-sub-saharan-africa/
94 http://www.africabusinesssource.com/articles/investment/can-obama-deliver-american-investment-in-africa/
95 http://www.fastcompany.com/magazine/126/special-report-china-in-africa.html
96 http://aidwatchers.com/2010/04/can-the-west-learn-from-china-in-africa/
97 http://www.ft.com/cms/s/0/ca3b7402-4b2e-11e0-911b-00144feab49a.html#axzz1GDetSqMa
98 http://www.ftadviser.com/FinancialAdviser/Pensions/News/article/20110310/e9f34bd8-4595-11e0-9885-00144f2af8e8/Corporate-pensions-deficit-reaches-1383bn-Xafinity.jsp
99 http://en.wikipedia.org/wiki/UK_miners%27_strike_%281984%E2%80%931985%29
100 http://en.wikipedia.org/wiki/Gordian_Knot

CHAPTER 4

FINANCIAL 'SERVICES'?

The future of money

Way back in 2007, I had the privilege of discussing the future of money at the Royal College of Art in London.

Based on what I considered to be the relevant drivers of change, the need to solve significant consumer problems from the consumers' point of view and likely sources of resistance to change, I suggested that the successful retail financial services of the future would:

- Leverage a shock amongst consumers who subsequently accept that the world has changed, yet help them to embrace that change;

- Solve the root cause of consumers' critical need in the course of actual or desired activities;

- Link with trusted third parties to provide a comprehensive consumer experience;

- Enable day-to-day control of the management of money with the consumer;

- Improve rapidly with user collaboration, giving value beyond the facilitator;

- Be safe, easy to use, and involve communications that are fair, transparent (enabling ready comparison) and neither misleading nor patronising;

- Continue to be enhanced by the facilitator to meet related consumer needs rather than to enrich facilitator itself;

- Play well with the regulators and public policy/opinion-formers;

- Not be offered by an entity that consumers perceive to be an 'institution'.

As a result, my prediction for 2008 in the Society for Computers and Law magazine was as follows:

> "Economic conditions will deteriorate further in the financial services industry. Downward pressure on revenue and the cost of funding, marketing and distributing financial services to consumers and small businesses will force institutions to compete on innovation and service quality. But not being organised to provide either, these incumbents will fail to resist the entry of facilitators that have built trust and loyalty by empowering consumers to get the product that is right for them personally in other retail markets. Banks will be the back office service providers, not the front, for Financial Services 2.0."

In February 2008, consultancy Gartner warned banks:[101]

> "not to attempt to copy social banking practices, unless they can clearly establish a strategic intent centred on social welfare, as opposed to traditional commercial return. Instead, banks should look to partner financial social networks, offering capabilities like transaction processing and risk management."

Of course, this was all pre-Lehman Brothers' collapse, but I wouldn't change a word today. The gap between our financial institutions and financial 'facilitators' has widened hugely since then.

This is partly because we don't bother switching banks[102] – so they see little point innovating to entice us and the profits are better spent cutting costs or finding new ways to charge fees. In November 2007, HSBC's chairman stated that retail banking "...is going to be less profitable than it is and is going to be growth constrained."[103] Since then, as we'll see in Chapter 5, UK banks have actually gone to court to defend fees that consumers and regulators have long complained are too high; have resisted for as long as possible the payment of claims for compensation for mis-selling payment protection insurance; and have tended to handle very high complaints levels very poorly. It's no surprise that the proportion of Britons still getting their financial advice from high street banks has declined from 28% in 2003 to just 4% in 2007.[104]

However, both the economic and regulatory environments have begun to favour non-banks that are closely aligned with their customers. In the UK, Tesco's buy-out of its joint venture with Royal Bank of Scotland is a prime example of commercial opportunism. And the advent of the Payment Services Directive is a good example of a regulatory bonus. That directive is aimed at removing EU banks' monopoly over payments, along with the time-lag in the movement of money through creaking legacy payment systems. The new rules have ushered in a wave of non-bank competitors which some banks are relieved to see. HSBC sold its acquiring arm to Global Payments, and EU state-aid rules forced bailed-out Royal Bank of Scotland to sell its acquiring arm to private investors in 2010.

Note, too, that both Google and Amazon have also added their own retail e-money offerings, alongside PayPal; and the use of Facebook Credits for purchases within the Facebook environment is booming.

Finally, as we shall see, the Basel III accord on bank capital requirements has not only forced banks to hoard capital rather than lend it; but the rules have also stiffened the headwind for banks in relation to riskier assets, such as unsecured personal loans and small business lending.

In November 2010, McKinsey reported[105] that banks will find it more costly and less profitable to offer short-term unsecured personal and small business finance under Basel III rules.

To comply with the new rules, banks face a long review of their businesses and products to reduce risk, use capital more efficiently and minimise the need for market funding by the end of 2012.

For these reasons, one might expect banks to allow their depositors to lend directly to their personal loan and small business customers. But it seems unlikely the banks could feed themselves on the scale of fees their nimble competitors can afford to charge. And they would soon face calls to allow the peer-to-peer approach for mortgages and larger corporate loans – by which time other more alert providers may well beat them to those segments too.

So it's no surprise there is demand for new and highly efficient e-finance platforms focused on personal loans, small business lending, social projects and equity fundraising.

Money – like music – is better shared

Here are my notes/thoughts from a discussion led by ethnographer Bruce Davis of Oikonomics[106] led on the notion that 'Finance is like the music industry in the '90s':

1   As individuals we actually share money, rather than 'consume' it. So we prefer to withhold it from those we perceive to be 'taking' our money and not sharing in return. Government and banks would fall into that category.

2   Recent events mean that our savings are perceived to be at risk, and not 'solid', even with the Financial Services Compensation Scheme guarantee.

3   Bankers' view of money has shifted in line with Greenspan's admission that his assumption about the efficiency of markets was wrong. As a result, banks no longer trust in the concept of sharing money and are hoarding it rather than lending it to their customers and other banks.

4   We agree the terms on which money is shared or used according to the context. That context may give money a very different meaning to the different participants (e.g. lender and borrower). On that basis, 'money' is not a static concept, but a dynamic. Similarly, some people view a loan as a cash float or a credit, rather than a debit or debt – e.g. a student loan. This is obviously frustrating to those with a traditional or accounting view of money, but has to be grasped to communicate effectively.

5 Focusing on our use of money, rather than its value, becomes instructive in figuring out the activities in which consumers are engaged when interacting with a financial services provider.

6 Trials have shown that if you remove the interest rates from the outside of a bank branch, footfall at that branch increases. Maybe the FSA and the OFT should focus more on the responsible/irresponsible uses of money, not advertised rates and other indicators of 'value'. Responsible lending/borrowing initiatives are the tip of the iceberg, since there are many other uses. On this basis it seems right that there is no usury cap in the UK, since the contextual use of the money, not the rate alone, is the most important issue.

7 It is perhaps worth considering that money is customary in very old economies, like the UK, not created, as it is in newer economies (including the US). Perhaps this entrenched custom is why, in the UK, there's a tendency to feel it's somehow 'wrong' to borrow, so we hide or ignore debt. This makes for worse over-indebtedness, whereas making debt visible leads people to try to pay it off.

8 Personally, we don't like being 'targeted' as 'consumers'. We prefer to be in control and demand products for our own reasons (which may change). On that basis providers should allow consumers to shape products.

9 Benefits tend to be presented as 'welfare' or public care. Recipients might feel more encouraged if the benefit or pension is styled as simply 'money' or an investment in them personally, or an attempt to provide capital, rather than merely 'care' which gets taken away if they find work or another source of income. There is a disincentive to return to work in that it takes so long to get back on benefits if you fail. Yet trial and failure – risk-taking – need to be encouraged for low income earners, as with any other form of entrepreneurship. Styling unemployment as a social issue closes off the economic, or entrepreneurial, path out of it.

10 Some risk is good, whereas our nanny state is committed to removing the risk from everything we do.

From the Pragmatist's standpoint, these are all great insights. Thinking of money as if it were music, like imagining your bank manager in underwear, may be a great way to demystify it. Currently it seems most people feel excluded by the formality and complexity associated with money. As a result, we don't even bother switching banks to get a better deal, let alone think about ways to use or share our money productively.

WeBank: new rules for the new economy

It was an encouragingly broad church that came to hear whether people will replace financial institutions at WeBank in January 2009 – more network economy than financial services.

While it was excellent to hear from platforms as diverse Zopa, Kubera Money and Midpoint & Transfer (a proposed P2P foreign exchange matching service), the panel discussion was also quite revealing.

For James Gardner, head of innovation in a bank, the question was whether peer-to-peer (P2P) finance would ever become so successful that it would make it uneconomic for banks to compete in the markets for deposits and personal loans.

Having spent considerable time trying to understand how P2P finance platforms will scale cost effectively, he doubted that banks will lose their grip on these markets. In particular, he felt that the cost of compliance with increasing regulation will constrain growth and fee income alone won't support the investment in resources required. However, various members of the audience were keen to point out that P2P finance is the product of a very different attitude to money than people's attitude to banking. For this reason the two should not be viewed merely in competitive terms.

Indeed, Giles Andrews (MD at Zopa), said Zopa lenders were not necessarily drawing on their savings, as opposed to investment capital, in their quest for greater personal control over their returns. However, Zopa was gradually taking market share from banks in personal loans, having disbursed about £31m,[107] and doubling volumes year on year. On this basis, Giles said there would be no problem with scalability.

Umair Haque of the Havas Media Lab sees P2P finance as a reflection that our established institutional rules have become ineffective, and must be re-written, in much the same way as other online marketplaces and social network services have introduced their own new rules, customs and etiquette. So we should look not so much at individual players or business models but at what set of rules is needed for social and economic recovery.

For my own part, I agree that P2P finance is not about 'banking'. They are on different, diverging paths.

But inevitably – and particularly in the current economic environment – one is drawn to the notion that banking as we have known it is doomed.

James Gardner's observation that banks can't see how P2P finance could possibly scale given current institutional constraints is quite telling. Perhaps it is that mindset that has given rise to frustration and innovation among non-banks, from hedge funds to payment service providers to retailers and even individual people. Everyone wants to do things differently to how banks insist they are done. Even formal regulation has opened up more lightly-regulated territory that was previously reserved for banks, such as e-money and payment service provision – tolerating non-regulated financial services at the same time.

In other words, the new economic rules are being written around banking, rather than by banks themselves.

Pay as you go financial services

Thanks to Dave Birch, of Consult Hyperion, for the link to the fascinating paper from May 2010 by Ignacio Mas and Dan Ratcliffe on the success of M-Pesa, the African payments system whose mission is to lower the cost of access to financial services.[108] I've updated some of the figures based on more recent reports, though none of them is as comprehensive.

The paper contains some great insights for serving both the 'unbanked' as well as other financial service customers. And I hadn't realised that the UK's Department for International

Development was instrumental in funding M-Pesa's initial development by staff from Vodafone and others.

As previous research for the UK's Financial Inclusion Taskforce demonstrated, the challenge of financial inclusion is not how to draw low income earners into the existing banking system, but how to make financial services more useful, convenient, cost effective and faster.[109] And that seems best encapsulated in 'pay as you go' models, since you 'know where you are' in terms of cost and usage/availability which is in itself convenient. M-Pesa makes an interesting case study because virtually all M-Pesa's 9m pay as you go users rate the service better than the alternatives on these factors. And that's not only the view of low income earners. The Mas and Ratcliffe report says M-Pesa users are more likely to have a bank account than non-users, as well as being wealthier, more literate, and better educated.

Here are some more stats from the report, as at January 2010 (except where stated):

- Users can cash-in/out at 16,900 retail stores [27,988 by April 2011][110] of which nearly half are located outside urban centres;

- There are US$320m per month in P2P transfers and US$650m per month in cash deposits and withdrawal transactions at M-PESA stores;

- The average transaction size is around US$33, but Vodafone has stated that half the transactions are for a value of less than US$10;

- US$7m in monthly revenue (based on the six months to September 2009);

- 27 companies use M-Pesa for bulk distribution of payments. Safaricom itself used it to distribute dividends on Safaricom stock to 180,000 individual shareholders who opted to receive their dividends into their M-Pesa accounts;

- Since March 2009, 75 companies [490 by May 2011][111] have used M-Pesa to collect bill payments from their customers.

About 20% of the electric utility's one million customers pay through M-Pesa;

- Two banks are using M-Pesa as a mechanism for customers to either repay loans or withdraw funds from their banks accounts.

While M-Pesa has been marketed very well, the report suggests the real key to its rapid, widespread adoption and frequent use is the decision to launch with a low-cost mobile payment infrastructure, rather than a savings or credit product. This allowed the business to follow the usage-based pre-paid mobile airtime model, so that each transaction was profitable from day one, and no potential customer or transaction size was excluded as 'unprofitable'. It's free to register and to pay money in, and there's no minimum balance. Now that so many people are on the system generating income, it's become easier and more cost effective to respond to their demand for other suitable financial services and functionality.

Banks, on the other hand, "tend to distinguish between profitable and unprofitable customers based on the likely size of their account balances and their ability to absorb credit." I'd suggest that not only does this mean banks need to limit their customer base and rate of service adoption, but having made so many assumptions about the services to be provided and customers who might want them, it also becomes ingrained that banks must control the product rather than allow customers to create and shape the services they want. For example, MetroBank's launch strategy assumed you want the same old banking services and delivery channels, but with merely longer branch opening hours, free coin-counting and immediate in-branch card delivery (oh, and dog food).[112] Hardly the 'revolution' it claims, compared to what's happening in Kenya.

The success of M-Pesa prompts comparisons with PayPoint, and how it's pragmatically solving parking payment problems using its PayByPhone service. And it's consistent with the adoption of prepaid cards, which aren't only for the unbanked, as Dave Birch has recently pointed out.[113] The Oyster card and O2 payment card are interesting examples, and 'my Travel Cash' from CorporatePay[114] was recommended by *Which?* in June 2011.[115] Away from payments, and at the higher end of the personal loan market, the pay as you go approach is reflected in Zopa's person-to-person lending fee structure: borrowers pay a one-off upfront fee with no charge for early repayment, and Zopa lenders only pay a servicing fee based on the amount they have lent out at any one time.

Of course, these fee structures are not to be confused with those direct debit payment plans that you see from the likes of utility companies and TV Licensing.[116] Those effectively deliver a lengthy advance payment or 'float' to the provider – or free working capital. Nice if you can get it, and a great example of a provider that is busy solving its own problem at the expense of its customers (or 'captives', in the case of TV Licensing).

Pay less, diversify more, be contrarian

John Kay's 'The Long and the Short of It' explains why retail investors should "pay less, diversify more, and be contrarian," without pushing some kind of snake oil that allegedly delivers the same financial result.[117] In fact, he says, "you are on your own" in the retail investment market. Which is not a great outcome after a decade of New Labour fiddling that was supposed to result in 'treating customers fairly'.

In essence, Kay explains that financial markets have a mind of their own, unrelated to fundamental value. Financial models that purport to predict performance over time may be illuminating but they are not true. He says, "frequent small gains [are] punctuated by occasional very large losses...", or 'Taleb distributions', as Nassim Nicolas Taleb explained in his books 'Fooled by Randomness' and 'The Black Swan'.

The market is fooled not only because faulty financial models are accepted as being more than merely illuminating, but also because competition amongst financial services firms based on relative performance moves markets "too far, too fast" for most participants to realise when to get out. To call a halt puts one's job at risk: "It is better to be conventionally wrong, than to be unconventionally right." So, while it pays the retail investor to *understand* the "mind of the market", your purpose in doing so is actually to *do the opposite* of what 'the market' is suggesting.

Interestingly, Kay's recommended regulatory response to the credit bubble is to "firewall the utility from the casino, by giving absolute priority to retail depositors...in the event of the failure of a deposit-taking institution." Yet, he adds:

> "The additional rules which will be introduced ... will be irrelevant to the next bubble, just as the Basel I and II capital requirements imposed on banks – the subject of so much regulatory and academic debate over the last two decades – were irrelevant to the credit bubble."

Maybe the financial regulators should simply dedicate themselves and their budgets to pushing the line:

> "You are on your own. Pay less. Diversify more. Be contrarian."

But there won't be very many international conferences or compliance jobs in that...

What's happening to my managed funds?

Heeding John Kay's warning, I've been paying a lot more attention to how much of my pension and ISA money is being left in the hands of so-called 'managers' who merely track (or underperform) an Index or their peers.

News on that front is getting worse.

According to the *FT*, fund managers are finding it tougher to gain distribution through European retail banks, which are the dominant sales channel in continental Europe. The banks are cutting the number of fund managers whose products they distribute, and the fund managers are "scrambling" to be included. "Some fund managers are likely to have to pay higher charges to distributors," the head of UK sales at JPMorgan Asset Management is quoted as saying. And the head of international retail business at BlackRock said: "Investors feel let down by what has happened in the financial sector as the industry has been focusing more on its own needs than those of clients."[118]

In the same article, Lipper estimates that UK retail banks only distribute about 4% of investment products sold in the UK, and IFA-advised sales remain dominant at about 53%. This news again signals the need to get more active, and use discount and execution-only providers to invest in cheaper products like basic Exchange Traded Funds.

This is not easy in the context of a full-time job and family commitments. My anxiety as a personal investor is rising at the same pace as the Eurozone debt balloon.

While I've previously used a discount investment broker and began a stakeholder-friendly pension, only recently have I woken up to the 'DIY ISA' and a low-cost self-invested personal pension (SIPP) that allows me to go 'off piste'. Next stop: ETFs in out-of-favour, non-correlated sectors.

WTFs, more like.

I do my best to keep track of various small investments in numerous pots that have accumulated over the years – several ISAs, pensions (corporate, SIPP and stakeholder-friendly) and child trust funds. I even move them around over the flames from time to time, in the hope that at least one or two will ignite... in a good way. But none has yet paved the way to retirement, let alone a comfortable one.

So what changes should I be making to my investment choices?

The first step in any such undertaking is to figure out exactly what each investment is worth, and whether I'm ahead or not. And that's where the whole personal investment management process comes to a juddering halt.

Figuring out whether your 10, 20 or 30 different funds actually represent a diversified portfolio, or ultimately all track each other, is no easy task for an amateur. And the pension trustees don't even suggest you try. Because not all of the relevant information is in the one place, and some of it is downright difficult to obtain, especially when one confronts the different ticker symbols that pension providers use, for example. And the annual statements from pension fund managers seem designed to prevent you from obtaining timely data on which you can act.

But let's face it, the product providers and IFAs can't really be expected to take a huge interest in your mish-mash of investments. They tend to earn fees simply based on how much of your money they have 'under management'. So if your investments are scattered to the four winds outside their control, the revenue they can earn from you is disproportionately small compared to the work required to pull all the performance data together. In fact, a cost-benefit analysis might tell you it's not worth paying anyone to do it at all. And that is the industry's hope, because it leaves management fee revenue with all those random providers from whom you fail to switch.

As we will see, the FSA has spent oodles of time and money reviewing retail distribution trying to improve the manner in which investment products are sold. But this ultimately seems an impossible task, given the current framework. The FSA's own 'MoneyMadeClear' website is like jargon soup. It has different tabs for pensions, as opposed to long-term savings and investments – when in all cases you might think you're simply 'investing for the future', and a good proportion of your money could end up in the same mutual fund or underlying shares. Worse, the FSA's review ignored any asset offered by a provider that it doesn't regulate, preventing it from seeing the financial world holistically, when we know that it's all hideously interconnected.

So what sort of investment service should one expect?

None – you're on your own, as John Kay explained. Yet I don't think I'm unrepresentative of a good many people over 40 who have a bunch of stray investments, and know they really ought to be doing something to keep it all under control. There must be a good market for a one-stop, low-cost service that would allow you to:

- Track all your savings and investments, whether in or outside pensions, taxable or non-taxable;
- Understand whether they're up, down or sideways;
- Benchmark them against competing options;
- Assess whether you are really diversified;

- Avoid the pitfalls of transfer fees, and dealing charges that hammer nails into some apparently cheap options (e.g. I'm told not to trickle money into ETFs); and

- Cost-effectively trade your way out of any holes.

All in a single afternoon.

Better still, the ideal service would tell you the impact of a particular asset on your portfolio as soon as you add it to your shopping basket.

The Diversification Challenge

There are numerous tips on how to make sure that 'not all your eggs are in one basket'. But they all assume that you have a lot of surplus cash, a great deal of time and a pretty sophisticated understanding of finance and financial services.

Yet, even with plenty of time on his/her hands, the 'man on the Clapham omnibus' is no financial giant.

So most people need diversification explained as simply as possible, and to be enabled to achieve it easily and conveniently.

What is diversification? The eggs in one basket idea is pretty simple, but needs some numbers: you are less likely to have all your eggs broken if you have 10 eggs in each of 10 baskets, rather than 100 eggs in one basket.[119] Following this principle, you become automatically better off every time you divide the same number of eggs among more baskets. So you're much better protected against egg breakage if you have five eggs in each of 20 baskets. For 'eggs', substitute asset classes – cash, bonds, houses, fine wine and so on.

An interesting challenge would be to start with what a truly diversified small portfolio of assets would look like. For argument's sake, one could start with a figure of £10,680[120] – the most the government allows you to salt away without locking it up until you're 98 years old, or paying tax on the returns.

But such government policy actually *prohibits* diversification, while heavily subsidising regulated investments at the expense of alternative, unregulated investments.

That's because most people with surplus cash should use up their tax-free allowances first, and few will have anything left over.[121] And the money allocated to those allowances cannot be invested in the full range of potential assets, even by putting money in the hands of fund managers. Generally, you may only invest your tax-free allowances in regulated investments. And all sorts of rules, policies and other restrictions limit the types of assets in which regulated fund managers can invest. So even regulated fund managers are unable to adequately diversify the investment pots they manage. This in turn exposes their performance to various adverse market-driven and/or behavioural effects.[122]

Then there's the tricky subject of asset correlation. If all the assets you've invested in behave the same way at the same time, they are highly correlated, meaning you aren't diversified, even though your eggs *seem* to be in different baskets. It's like the baskets are stacked on top of one another, moving up and down in unison. That has become more of a problem in the past few years, because all our savings and investment money has been chasing the same allegedly safe regulated assets.[123] Of course, that won't continue forever, and no doubt the herd will be caught out horribly when 'discorrelation' occurs.[124]

Still with me?

While they are discriminated against in terms of tax subsidies, unregulated alternative investments will remain beyond the reach of most people. The rich, on the other hand, are able to invest more widely which makes their portfolios automatically more valuable and better protected when some of their investments turn sour. The regulators regard them as 'sophisticated investors' who are able to look after themselves – and they certainly do. I'm sure that senior banking executives, regulatory officials and politicians are all well represented in this class.

Worse still, the effective prohibition on diversification is deeply entrenched. As we'll see in Chapter 5, our financial regulatory framework is so hard-wired in favour of the status quo it takes an inordinate amount of time and persistence to obtain regulated status for a truly alternative investment.

So how could we enable ordinary people to put their eggs in more baskets?

First, we should figure out a reasonably detailed list of asset classes; then we should modify the regulatory framework to enable people to invest at least their tax-free allowance in each of them. I've made some regulatory suggestions in Chapter 5. In the meantime, for the sake of argument, I've suggested a reasonably full list of asset classes below. To most people, the list will be gobbledygook and we definitely need a way to explain the differences simply. However, we have to start somewhere. Note that I've included different types of 'funds', and separated those that are regulated from those which aren't, because their performance can be affected by the differing levels of regulation and permitted classes of investments they can make. I haven't included derivative contracts.

Am I right or wrong? How would you suggest we meet the 'Diversification Challenge'? The list is as follows:

1   Cash

2   Savings accounts with regulated financial institutions

3   Fixed interest savings/bonds – government

4   Fixed interest savings/bonds – corporate

5   Person-to-person loans

6   Shares listed on a regulated or 'recognised' exchange

7   Shares not listed on a regulated exchange

8   Exchange traded funds (ETFs) listed on a regulated exchange

9   ETFs not listed on a regulated exchange

10   Regulated managed funds

11   Unregulated managed funds

12   Regulated hedge funds

13   Unregulated hedge funds

14   Venture capital funds

15   Venture capital trusts

16 Regulated funds of funds

17 Unregulated funds of funds

18 Commercial property

19 Rural property

20 Residential property (owner occupied)

21 Residential property (buy-to-let)

22 Perishable commodities (e.g. cocoa, wheat)

23 Non-perishable commodities (e.g. oil, gold and other precious metals)

24 Art

25 Classic cars

26 Fine wine

27 Currencies

The role of social media in financial services

I laughed when it was suggested that Twitter was somehow failing because only 10% of people on Twitter are responsible for 90% of the content, based on "a snapshot of 300,542 users in May 2009."[125]

Twitter is a highly efficient way for people to engage with each other, either by publishing their observations or reading those of others, in a bite-size format. This utility is reflected in the report that "visitors to the site increased by 1,382%, from 475,000 to seven million, between February 2008 and February 2009" against Facebook's 228% growth for a similar period. Since then, Twitter has gone on to announce 100m active users, averaging 230m tweets a day, and estimates that it will add another 26m users by January 2012.[126] It doesn't matter if most people 'lurk'. Lurking is good. To put that in context, Kim Tasso[127] recently said that she'd been worried when only three people were tweeting from a legal conference she was attending. Until she realised 40 people had subscribed to one of the feeds.

But you can't analyse Twitter in isolation, or say that it's really competing against anything or anyone. Twitter is not a divisible or competitive 'channel' or medium. It's merely part of a cooperative mix of many different types of web site that are increasingly inter-linked and intertwined, enabling access to content from different people at different times on different platforms and networks, depending on where people are and what they're doing.

All of which is to say that Twitter – like any one of the other sub-networks on the Internet – is the tip of a giant iceberg.

Interestingly, James Gardner, then the head of innovation and research in a major UK bank, said in 2009 that, for banks, Twitter is a stunt.[128] He said it was uneconomic for a bank to commu-nicate through the medium because – I hope I don't summarise unfairly – it's too expensive for banks to create content that's rele-vant to people at scale. "Surely no one," he said, "thinks Twitter is going to be a *channel choice* that many customers are going to use regularly."

It's true that banks haven't really done much on Twitter (nor innovated in the consumer product space at all), but Twitter's meteoric growth figures show how tough it is to predict people's 'channel choice'. Human physiology may be reasonably predict-able, but human behaviour is not. This is Black Swan territory. In reality, there is no 'mass' of consumers, no bell-curve to accurately describe their behaviour or enable us to predict with any *precision* how each person is likely to behave next. We are merely guessing, because there is a point at which all the credit scoring and other 'models' break down.[129]

Twitter – or Facebook, for that matter – could disappear in a sudden puff of user indifference, like others before it, and every-one could migrate to something new that they regard as more usable or useful. Keep your eye on Google+[130]…

So where does this leave financial services?

As explained in earlier chapters, because the social media seem to reflect a rising desire to structure our personal lives and experi-ences as each of us sees fit, the best way to facilitate that desire for personal control is by providing financial services that are highly flexible and adaptable, bottom-up from the user level, rather than by dictating how services must work in a top-down fashion.

That means mapping the steps in customers' end-to-end activities and figuring out which steps you can facilitate, and where you need to cooperate with other providers to supply a seamless service. It means recognising which stage of that activity the customer is engaged in when using your service, where he's obtaining information about your products and even what stage of the 'change curve' that activity represents.

In this context, it's worth noting that Zopa members moderate their discussion boards rather than Zopa staff. And Zopa encourages members to use Twitter for informal requests, queries or non-sensitive admin, because it's faster and more accessible, efficient and transparent than email.

In this environment it's an incredibly brave yet foolhardy commercial decision for any business to ignore Twitter or any other social media, even if only 10% of users generate 90% of the content.

---

101 http://www.finextra.com/news/fullstory.aspx?newsitemid=18049

102 Bank current accounts and credit products, investments, pensions and securities all feature in the bottom 20% of the European Commission's 'Market Performance Indicator', with investments, pensions and securities coming in lucky last. Only 34% of consumers think they deliver what's promised. Yet 76% of us don't bother to switch providers.

103 http://www.ft.com/cms/s/0/998156fa-9a02-11dc-ad70-0000779fd2ac.html?nclick_check=1

104 http://www.ft.com/cms/s/0/5e9d97e4-c7c3-11dc-a0b4-0000779fd2ac.html

105 http://www.mckinseyquarterly.com/Basel_III_Now_the_hard_part_for_European_banks_2704

106 http://www.oikonomics.typepad.com/

107 Zopa lenders advanced £70m in 2010; and are estimated to advance £140m in 2011: http://thefinanser.co.uk/fsclub/2011/10/10-of-lending-via-p2p.html

108 http://pymnts.com/mobile-payments-go-viral-m-pesa-in-kenya/

109 http://webarchive.nationalarchives.gov.uk/20100104214853/http:/hm-treasury.gov.uk/d/bmrb_research.pdf

110 http://www.safaricom.co.ke/index.php?id=1073

111 http://kopokopo.tumblr.com/post/6718211777/safaricom-m-pesa-room-to-grow

112 http://www.hillingdontimes.co.uk/news/localnews/9333607.New_Uxbridge_bank_boasts_longer_later_hours/

113 http://www.chyp.com/media/blog-entry/i-love-prepaid-but-not-everyone-does

114 A client.

115 http://corporatepay.co.uk/news_media/which.html

116 http://www.tvlicensing.co.uk/pay/payment-methods/viewpaymentcontent.aspx?id=pay1&iqdocumentid=pay1

117 J. Kay, *The Long and the Short of It: A Guide to Finance and Investment for Normally Intelligent People Who Aren't in the Industry*, The Erasmus Press, 2009

118 http://www.ft.com/cms/s/e5a35008-3685-11de-af40-00144feabdc0, Authorised=false.html?_i_location=http%3A%2F%2Fwww.ft.com%2Fcms%2Fs%2F0%2Fe5a35008-3685-11de-af40-00144feabdc0.html&_i_referer=http%3A%2F%2Fsearch.ft.com%2Fsearch%3FqueryText%3Dfunds%2Bto%2Bcompete%2Bfor%2Bbank%2Bpartners%26x%3D0%26y%3D0

119 http://en.wikipedia.org/wiki/Diversification

120 http://www.hmrc.gov.uk/budget2011/tiin9375.pdf

121 Research cited by the Guardian in June 2011 suggests the average UK person can afford to save £97.10 per month: http://www.guardian.co.uk/money/2011/jun/07/half-uk-not-saving-retirement

122 http://blog.iii.co.uk/the-rediscovered-benjamin-graham/

123 E.g.http://ftalphaville.ft.com/blog/2009/06/30/59661/investors-go-moo/; and http://ftalphaville.ft.com/blog/2011/10/13/701651/sp-takes-away-cdo-diversification-candy/

124 http://ftalphaville.ft.com/blog/2009/09/25/74056/discorrelation-alert/?source=rss

125 http://news.bbc.co.uk/1/hi/technology/8089508.stm

126 http://www.guardian.co.uk/technology/pda/2011/sep/08/twitter-active-users

127 http://www.kimtasso.com

128 http://bankervision.typepad.com/bankervision/2009/04/for-banks-twitter-is-a-stunt.html

129 'Metaphors, Models and Theories' by Emanuel Derman, author of 'My Life as a Quant', currently a professor at Columbia University and the head of risk at a fund manager (http://papers.ssrn.com/sol3/papers.cfm?abstract_id=1713405). I reviewed it at: http://sdj-pragmatist.blogspot.com/2011/01/of-models-and-short-regulators.html

130 https://plus.google.com/

CHAPTER 5

FINANCIAL REGULATION PROTECTS
INSTITUTIONS AT OUR EXPENSE

As we've seen so far, our financial system is geared to suit financial institutions, whereas it should enable customers to pay less and diversify more via simple, low-cost financial services. This chapter is based on a series of posts[131] which identify the relevant flaws in the regulatory framework, and why well-intentioned attempts to simplify financial products have failed to date. It examines the complex world of 'shadow banking' and ends with a suggested alternative regulatory model for retail finance that should facilitate, rather than inhibit, consumer empowerment.

Of creative destruction, auditors and rating agencies

Among the lessons to be learned from the financial crisis, we've not heard much about how the market for audit services and credit ratings will change to help protect taxpayers from footing the bill for future bail-outs.

There have been many significant accounting scandals in the past decade. Enron died in 2001, eventually taking accounting giant Arthur Andersen with it. WorldCom filed for Chapter 11 bankruptcy in 2002, the same year the Tyco scandal broke. In 2003, the Ahold and Parmalat scandals surfaced. In 2004, it was AIG under investigation, which duly restated its net worth as being 3.3% lower than investors had been led to believe.

In the meantime, Madoff's activities went unchecked until 2008 and investment banks packaged the riskiest types of mortgages into allegedly low-risk bonds, seriously undermining confidence in the standards set by rating agencies.

More scandals and 'surprise losses' are on the way. Internal auditors at 75 major UK corporations recently confessed that they are failing to stem the rising tide of fraud, and are increasingly vulnerable to it:

> "The three most common types of fraud were misappro-priation of assets, suffered by 31% of companies, improper expenditures (22%) and procurement fraud at 16%. Poor financial controls and collusion between employees and third parties were seen as important drivers of fraud."[132]

From these cases one might conclude that accounting, financial controllership, auditing and the assessment of credit risk have all succumbed to the same illness. At any rate, lack of clear lines of demarcation or clarity on cause and effect suggest there are more similarities than differences between the activities of rating agencies and audit firms, so they ought to share each other's criticism. Only four firms audit most of our major corporations, including banks, while only three rating agencies assess the risk of default on most of planet Earth's 'investment grade' securities. As a result debate rages as to where the scope of external audit responsibility begins and ends, and whether firms who offer audit services should be free to offer accounting, regulatory and risk management advice – or, indeed, credit ratings. According to Reuters, the European Commission may propose a new law banning the Big Four's ability to audit while providing consulting services to their clients or face being broken up, and the Public Company Accounting Oversight Board may require mandatory auditor rotations to fend off complacency.[133]

But surely we can't continue to overlook the fundamental conflict in auditors and rating agencies purporting to 'independently' verify the activities of the corporations who pay their fees – especially when auditors need to be schooled in the meaning of 'scepticism'. Interestingly, in May 2010 it was reported that two of the Big Four major global audit firms suggested they were planning to launch rating businesses. However, "John Griffith Jones, chairman of KPMG UK, said while starting a credit rating arm was a 'plausible' move, fears of conflicts of interest 'probably makes it impractical.'"[134]

Little wonder that the Financial Reporting Council's Professional Oversight Board believes that the Big Four accounting firms outweigh their regulatory constraints. And that the G20 leaders wish to reduce their reliance on ratings, while global regulators have called for an alternative to single-grade ratings by rating agencies. In addition, EU legislation was proposed in November 2011 to:

- Reduce reliance on ratings;
- Increase competition and elimination of conflicts of interest;
- Increase transparency and rigour in the rating of sovereign debt; and
- Create a European framework for civil liability in the case of serious misconduct or gross negligence.[135]

Experience suggests that these sorts of issues are only addressed after a directly related crisis has occurred – the process of creative destruction traced by Niall Ferguson in 'The Ascent of Money'. Unfortunately, while Arthur Andersen did not survive the Enron scandal, structural issues in the audit and ratings markets did.

So I guess there'll be a lot more destruction before these problems are resolved...

Should regulators be short?

As the ebbing economic tide exposes more and more fraud, it's striking to see how long the authorities have been aware of some problems before attempting to correct or publicise them.

But how are investors protected in the meantime?

Shouldn't investors be given a chance to cut their losses and switch to better investments as soon as problems are detected? Shouldn't new investors be compensated for transactions they would not have entered into had they been aware of the misconduct or a firm's diminished reputation?

A review of various accounting, debt and pension scandals suggests that, rather than banning short-selling "to protect the integrity and quality of the securities market and strengthen investor confidence",[136] regulators would be more effective if they were to use or *publicise* short selling as a tool to identify and punish errant firms and companies and to *promote* market confidence.

Lack of timely regulatory response to financial problems is perhaps best illustrated in books like 'Fooling Some of the People All of the Time' about the six years of foot-dragging over Allied Capital's creative accounting and 'The Big Short', about the few players who figured out there was a sub-prime debt crisis using publicly available data long before regulators realised there was a problem. It's also emerged what a poorly kept secret Madoff's fraud was, yet nothing was done officially until it was too late. And Ernst and Young have been taken to task over Lehman's use of so-called 'Repo 105' transactions to take certain assets off its balance sheet at each quarter-end.[137] Other specific examples have been given in defence of short-selling before.

Some recent examples closer to home are also instructive.

In May 2009, Aegon (then known as Scottish Equitable) informed the FSA of 300 'issues' amounting to £60m of consumer detriment. Yet this was only presented to the marketplace on 16 December 2010, with a 30% reduction in Aegon's fine, from £4m to £2.8m. In April 2010 various trading firms were fined £4.2m, for failing to "provide accurate and timely transaction reports to the FSA." Yet only now are we told that:

> "Each firm could have prevented the breaches by carrying out regular reviews of its data. *Despite repeated reminders from the FSA during the course of 2007 and 2008,* none of the firms did this."[138]

While civil enforcement authorities tiptoe around the edges of market problems, things are no better on the criminal enforcement side. UK judges are understandably reluctant to approve US-style 'plea bargains' that result in smaller fines and no admission of illicit conduct. A recent case in point was Mr Justice Bean's adverse reaction to the tiny 'settlement' to emerge from the notorious BAE Systems saga.[139]

Why all this regulatory timidity?

One justification is that it encourages firms to report their own misdeeds rather than hide them. Yet once it is reported privately by the miscreant the misconduct *does* remain hidden from customers and investors *by the regulators*. And informal regulatory discussions can be problematic. Witness the concern around the *FT's* report that UK banks' auditors may have factored assurances of government support into their opinions as to whether the banks were going concerns in 2008. Worryingly, the *FT* notes that "auditors are likely to be encouraged to have more private chats with regulators to help prevent another crisis."[140] Remember these are the guys who are having trouble understanding the role of scepticism in the audit context!

In cases of corporate fraud, the justification for restraint is similarly misplaced, as David Einhorn explains in 'Fooling Some of the People All of the Time':

> "The authorities really don't know what to do about fraud when they discover it *in progress*... It seems the regulatory thinking... is that shareholders should not be punished for corporate fraud, because... they are the victims in the first place... This thinking may be politically expedient in the short term, but creates a classic moral hazard – a free fraud zone. If regulators insulate shareholders from the penalties of investing in corrupt companies, then investors have no incentive to demand honest behaviour and worse, no need to avoid investing in dishonest companies... If investors believe that companies making false and misleading statements will be punished, they will be more sensitive to what is said [and] allocate their capital more carefully. This sensitivity and other consequences will, in turn, deter dishonesty."

And what sort of people will be attracted to corporate boards if they know that the authorities will always act to shield investors from their own flaky due diligence in the face of fraud? Sy Jacobs perhaps put it best:

> "Any business where you can sell a product and make money without having to worry how the product performs is going to attract sleazy people..."[141]

As we'll see shortly, regulators also cite their own statutory boundaries as the basis for ignoring firms' shadow banking activities. This may be a good technical defence, but feeble given that the shadow and traditional financial markets are interconnected globally, the former dwarfs the regulated sphere and is populated by subsidiaries of traditional bank holding companies.

Finally, unlike a typical approach to risk assessment, the authorities are not legally entitled to extrapolate from problems found in a sample of enforcement cases to reach a view on a 'portfolio basis'.[142]

So I wonder whether short sellers have something to teach regulators? If regulators were to publish the material facts triggering enforcement cases or even publicise applicable short positions, wouldn't investors be able to decide for themselves?

What distinguishes the short sellers' approach from the enforcement process?

The literature suggests that, first, short sellers think more deeply and critically than the financial authorities about the limits of the various models used in and around the financial markets. As Emanuel Derman has explained:

> "Models are analogies, and always describe something *relative* to something else. Theories, in contrast (sic) are *the real thing*. They don't compare; they describe the essence, without reference... There are no genuine theories in finance... Only imperfect models remain."[143]

Everyone is operating on models – rating models, asset pricing and valuation models, accounting models that assume a company's health is reflected in its financial statements, regulatory models that may be either 'light touch' or heavily prescriptive. Yet these models ultimately only 'bite' or affect the price when a transaction occurs. And since transactions only occur between buyers and sellers, only *their* beliefs about how models 'work' affect each transaction. The authorities and control functions remain on the sidelines. So the 'protective' models deployed by support functions and regulators can only be effective if they are properly deployed and fully understood by buyers and sellers. This seems impracticable, given that regulators, lawyers, accountants, rating agency managers and bond traders have very different views of the same market, and differing attitudes to their employers, clients and so on.

Second, once short sellers detect a potential anomaly, they investigate it with a view to trading – putting themselves at real risk – potentially over a long period of time. Whereas the authorities merely investigate to determine whether or not to activate a more formal, lengthy investigation, which might eventually end in a secondary enforcement process. That process might in turn end in a fine or settlement without any admission of wrongdoing. So short sellers are driven by a strong sense of anxiety about being wrong, while the authorities are not.

Ultimately we have a choice either to improve the knowledge of market participants relative to the complexity of products (through more transparency, better education and training and/ or by reducing the complexity of the products) or for regulators to play a more active role in transactions. The latter seems more practicable.

Publicising adverse material facts or relevant short positions may be a controversial regulatory tool. But adopting the same disciplines as the most sceptical market participants would help to remove the time lag and lack of transparency associated with civil and criminal actions.

We expect too much of regulators

The Financial Services Authority's own internal audit report into the mis-handling of Northern Wreck[144] signalled deep internal problems and recommended improvements on virtually all fronts. But those recommendations came eight years and too many financial scandals into that agency's existence to ensure its survival.

Yet the UK government has merely shuffled the regulatory deckchairs by passing the bulk of the FSA's consumer protection responsibility (and a good many staff) to a 'new' Financial Conduct Authority (FCA). Similarly, the objectives that have been set for the FCA don't seem to add much, and may best be described in this context as 'vague' or even 'feeble' (though others may complain this gives the FCA unbridled discretion). The FCA will have the single 'strategic' objective of "protecting and enhancing confidence in the UK financial system" and three 'operational' objectives:

- Securing an appropriate degree of protection for consumers;

- Promoting efficiency and choice in the market for financial services; and

- Protecting and enhancing the integrity of the UK financial system.

The FCA's obligations are equally vague. It must, "so far as is compatible with its objectives, discharge its general functions in a way which promotes competition...." and it is required "to have regard to the importance of taking action intended to minimise the extent to which regulated businesses may be used for a purpose connected with financial crime." Finally, the FCA must "have regard to six regulatory principles:

- The need to use its resources in the most efficient and economic way;

- Proportionality, the principle that a burden or restriction imposed on a person or activity should be proportionate to the benefits which are expected to result;

- The general principle that consumers should take responsibility for their decisions;

- The responsibilities of senior management to comply with the regulatory framework;

- Openness and disclosure, publishing information about regulated persons or requiring them to publish information...; and

- That the FCA should exercise its functions as transparently as possible...."

To be fair, significant opportunities for improvement may come from focusing on the root cause of consumer distress, rather than relying only on point-of-sale conduct and complaints (although I

don't understand why this could not have been done by the FSA
long ago):

> "Drawing on the work of the new business and market analy-
> sis team and analysis of business models, the FCA will base
> its regulatory interventions on a deeper understanding of
> underlying commercial and behavioural drivers and the often
> multiple causes of poor outcomes for consumers. *This will
> involve analysis of often complex chains of interaction. It could
> include reaching up the distribution chain, where appropriate,
> to intervene in wholesale activity where this could be the source
> of significant retail detriment.* This will fully reflect the FCA's
> increased focus on promoting competition and in securing
> the right outcomes for consumers. It will be an important
> change in regulatory approach." [My emphasis added]

It remains to be seen what the FCA will *do* with all this analytical
data. Without an astronomical and growing budget, the FCA will
never be able to hire enough people of sufficient calibre, and keep
them sufficiently trained and informed, to detect every significant
hole in firms' evolving business plans/models or all the services
that exploit rather than facilitate consumer behaviour. And even
if the FCA could meet those challenges, the chances of it actually
persuading regulated firms' management to accept that a particular hole exists, or that a certain service is exploitative, and to
redress the problem quickly enough, seem very unlikely to work
every time. After all, participating in financial markets inherently
involves the assumption of risk, not completely eliminating it.

Worse, the FCA won't have any remit to consider the impact
of activities that it does not regulate, just as the activities in the
shadow banking system escaped its predecessor.

Finally, experience tells us that it will be impossible to genuinely measure the FCA's performance against its objectives and
obligations – but we'll certainly know any gross failures when we
see them. [See text box.]

A proud history of mis-selling

Let's look at how effectively the existing regulatory framework has protected consumers by focusing on the most recent mis-selling 'scandal' and panning out to the wider context.

From 2000 to 2005 over 5m payment protection insurance (PPI) policies were sold to consumers in the UK – a market worth over £7bn a year.[145]

In June 2008, the FSA fined Alliance & Leicester £7m for mis-selling 210,000 PPI policies from January 2005 to December 2007 at an average price of £1,265. It found there had been "a general failure by advisers to give customers details of the cost of PPI... [and] A&L sought to find reasons to sell PPI without properly considering what customers needed." Meanwhile, the Competition Commission also alleged that consumers were being overcharged £1.4bn a year for PPI policies. But when the Competition Commission called for a ban on the sale of PPI with other financial products in November 2008, major lenders smugly warned that this would simply increase the cost of those products – clearly indicating massive cross-subsidies from the sale of PPI, meaning big profits. In December 2008, the FSA fined Egg £721,000, for mis-selling 106,000 PPI policies to its card customers at an average of £156 each for the period January 2005 to December 2007.

Finally, in January 2009, Alliance & Leicester, Barclays, the Co-operative Bank, Lloyds Banking Group (including Lloyds TSB, Halifax and Bank of Scotland), and RBS/NatWest announced they would halt the sale of single premium PPI (where the customer pays the whole premium up-front). Tellingly, in their mid-2011 financial reports, the major UK banks reported huge provisions for compensation to the victims of PPI mis-selling: Lloyds Banking Group, £3.2bn; Royal Bank of Scotland, £850m; Barclays, £1bn; Santander, £538m; and HSBC, £270m. In all, the FSA claims that "tough enforcement action was taken against 24 firms." Yet those banks had enjoyed the use of their victims' money for 11 years before finally being shamed into providing for its return – which is not to say it's all been repaid yet.

This would be shocking enough if mis-selling PPI had been the authorities' first experience of mis-selling retail financial services within the regulated sector. But it wasn't.

In 1994, the Securities and Investment Board (later subsumed into the FSA) finally woke up to the fact that:

> "Between 1988 and 1994 millions of consumers were advised to take out personal pension plans when they were already members of, or had access to, an occupational defined benefit pension scheme. In addition, many employees who had preserved pensions with the scheme of a former employer were advised to transfer into a personal pension scheme. Much of this advice was unsuitable, generating commission for advisers but reducing benefits for transferees... That exercise ultimately resulted in over £10bn of redress to consumers, at great financial and reputational cost to the industry and regulators. It damaged consumer confidence and caused years of anxiety to millions of consumers."[146]

Similarly, the Personal Investment Authority (also subsumed into the FSA) reluctantly acknowledged the mis-selling of about 12m mortgage endowment policies from the 1970s until the market collapsed in the 1990s. It found there had been "weak disclosure of the risk that investments might not cover the mortgage, and little consideration of suitability." Only £3bn of redress was paid to consumers and enforcement actions totalled a mere £10m of fines – an average of less than £1 for every policy sold.

In February 2009, whistle-blower Paul Moore gave us some great insights into the culture at a UK retail bank during the credit boom, and how that may have affected the FSA's outlook. In summary, Moore's evidence was that HBOS's then CEO, Sir James Crosby, had personally sacked Moore for persistently raising concerns about the bank's aggressive lending policies. The day after that evidence was given to a Parliamentary committee, Crosby resigned as deputy chairman of the FSA.

In June 2009, it was announced that UK banks would lose their self-regulatory control over deposits, savings and payments products *yet retain control of lending and credit card standards,* including standards governing the treatment of customers in financial difficulties.[147] That carve-out reflected the FSA's haughty aversion to regulating consumer credit, which is governed by the Consumer Credit Act 1974 – a nightmarish quagmire of complexity and foolishness cobbled together during decades of bitter squabbling amongst banks, politicians and consumer groups, which the OFT had failed to police effectively. Clearly this was a nettle that no one was willing to grasp, even though banks have hardly distinguished themselves by managing their own credit standards. Since then, the new UK government has sensibly consulted on moving responsibility for consumer credit under the FCA, but has yet to announce its decision.[148]

In July 2009, the last UK government belatedly issued 'A Better Deal for Consumers',[149] a white paper calling for an end to the bank charges litigation (explained below), a ban on sending unsolicited credit card cheques, and (shamed by a US credit card crackdown) threatening restrictions on re-pricing credit cards after they've been issued and the removal of the 'negative payment hierarchy', which prevented cardholders from paying off the highest rate items on their card bills first. Since then there has been a steady stream of stories about poor retail banking behaviour:

- Lloyds Banking Group announced a provision of £500m for payments to 600,000 mortgage borrowers who were 'confused' about their interest rate;

- Barclays Bank confirmed its withdrawal from asset-based small business lending, explaining that its "proposition was not that compelling, comprehensive [or] competitive" and that it wasn't commercially worthwhile to spend money on compliance or other necessary improvements;

- RBS and NatWest were fined £5.6m in relation to customer due diligence checks;

- HSBC has been revealed to have made a disastrous foray into the US mortgage market) and to have perhaps known a little more about 'the magic of Madoff'[150] than it let on to its clients;

- RBS was fined £2.8m for poor complaints handling;

- Barclays was fined £7.7m for investment advice failings and withdrew investment advisory services from its branches;

- Lloyds Banking Group agreed to pay compensation of £17m to customers whose complaints were among the half that were wrongly rejected in relation to HBOS investment products;

- Barclaycard curbed its sales of 'identity theft protection insurance' at £80 a year, following news of the FSA's investigation into the product provider, CPP; and

- Competition authorities globally continue to push for curbs on interchange fees from which credit card and debit card issuers benefit in connection with retail sales.

The bank that's fair?

The Financial Services Consumer Panel, an independent statutory consumer body, has reported that "Financial services compare poorly to the retail sector, with consumers considering financial services as less fair, being insufficiently competitive or accessible."[151]

Hey, *life* is unfair, I hear you say. Why does fairness matter here?

Well, apart from the massive difference in bargaining power between a national or global financial institution and the average person, UK banks rely on taxpayer support of at least £512bn, according to the National Audit Office.[152] And that doesn't include the cost of ring-fencing retail bank activities, as recommended by the Independent Commission on Banking, the impact of any further deterioration in the economy, the ability for individuals to offset trading profits against losses on regulated investments, nor the tax subsidy banks receive in the form of the £350bn Individual Savings Account programme.[153] Banks are accused of abusing this last privilege, in particular, by offering a mere 0.41% average interest rate on ISA cash deposits, after high 'teaser' rates expire.

Other research has found a spread of about 11% between UK bank savings and loans.[154]

It's one thing to avert an overnight systemic failure with public money, but it doesn't seem 'fair' to prop-up exploitative, inefficient business models over the longer term.

The broader economics aside, we also gained a fascinating cultural insight into banks' view of what is 'fair' during a series of court actions in which seven major banks resisted the OFT's jurisdiction to assess the 'fairness' of £2.6bn a year in overdraft charges.[155] The OFT was concerned because about 20% of current account customers with an overdraft facility generate enough income to pay for the entire UK current account system (and no doubt a handsome profit). Furthermore, the OFT didn't think consumers really had a choice of products or providers:

> "The complexity and lack of transparency of personal current accounts makes it extremely difficult for individual customers to compare their bank account with other offers. There is thus little incentive for consumers to switch – especially as people generally believe that it is complex and risky to switch accounts. Also, when the switching process does go wrong consumers can find themselves bearing a significant proportion of the resulting costs. The result is that only 6% of customers we surveyed had switched in the last 12 months – one of the lowest switching rates in Europe."[156]

The Financial Ombudsman Service (FOS), the financial services complaints watchdog, was awash with complaints about various overdraft-related charges, but felt obliged to patiently awaiting the outcome of the banks' challenge to the OFT's complaint before processing them. In turn, this encouraged numerous opportunistic 'claims management' providers to promise alternative means of resolving the issue at great expense, when FOS's service is free to consumers. In October 2008, the consumer body *Which?* said that for banks to fight the OFT's right to assess the fairness of these charges in the current economic circumstances, was "piling on the misery" for those affected.

Finally, in September 2009 – three years after the OFT's initial complaint, bailed-out Royal Bank of Scotland announced that it would halve its fee for paying an item when overdrawn *to £15 per day*, and slash the fee for returning a cheque, direct debit or standing order to £5 *(from £38!)*. Others followed suit.

How was that process fair?

Policy fail? Simple products and HM Treasury

In 2010, the Centre for Policy Studies reported that "long-term savings are overly complex, with multiple tax regimes that deter people from saving."[157] The report continued:

> "The pension and savings industry has suffered a near fatal erosion of trust, fuelled by mis-selling scandals, excessive costs and a long period of poor investment returns. This has catalysed a regulatory backlash."

Even the regulators are victims – not only of the subversive activities of their own regulated firms, but also of the sheer complexity of the regime. Witness the virtual swamp, for example, that is the FSA's ironically-named 'Money Made Clear' web site.

While proposals to simplify financial regulation remain preoccupied with financial services themselves – arbitrary product categories, mystifying jargon and random pots and limits – the situation will only become worse.

According to a report by Professor James Devlin for the UK Treasury, regulated financial services providers have failed to cooperate with various government initiatives to encourage the offering of simple financial products.[158] In relation to low-cost pensions, for example, he found that:

> "The combination of a relatively low fee cap [1–1.5%], free movement in and out of products without penalty and the relatively low level of funds invested by many users together represented a formidable barrier to enthusiasm from the industry for previous 'simple products.'"

The lack of simple regulated financial products affects virtually the entire UK population. Yes, the primary target of 'simple product' initiatives may be people earning less than £30,000 a year, with little interest or expertise in financial services and/or limited savings. But even people on *higher* incomes say they'd welcome "standards which show when a financial service offers customers a reasonable deal". Presumably, this includes the 4.3m owner-operated small and medium-sized businesses in the UK.

And, as the Treasury noted in the accompanying consultation on simple financial products: 48% of UK households have less than a month's salary in savings, and 27% have none at all.[159]

When launching the Retail Distribution Review of financial advice in 2006, the FSA claimed that "insufficient consumer trust and confidence in the products and services supplied by the market lie at the root of what we are seeking to address." And while Professor Devlin cites research to the effect that trust in financial service providers is "not significantly below" supermarkets, mobile phone providers and the NHS, that's not saying very much. Only 19% of us think the banks are run well, down from 90% in 1983 and 60% in 1994.[160] Investments, pensions and securities are also the least trusted consumer services across the EU.[161] Only 34% of consumers think the services deliver what's promised, 26% of us are as likely to trust investment providers as used car salesmen, yet 76% of us don't bother to switch providers. I mean, what would be the point?

Faced with regulated financial services providers' continuing refusal to supply suitable investment, pension and savings products at reasonable prices, you'd think the government would directly question the structure of *all* the providers and their products, like the broad base of 'vanilla products' proposed in the US (meeting strong resistance from providers, of course).

Instead, however, in launching its consultation on the development of simple financial products, the UK government rather meekly focused on simplifying 'deposit savings accounts' and *income protection insurance*:

> "Although the Government believes that the principles of simple products are widely applicable, it also believes that, initially, simple products should focus on products that do not carry risk to capital, i.e. that are not investment products. Risk would add an extra level of complexity to the product design, as the design would have to weigh up how much risk

individuals are willing to bear, both in terms of capital risk
and risk to gains."[162]

This astonishingly narrow focus fails on at least four counts.
First, and most obviously, it shies away from the distinct lack of
simple investment products and leaves the job of risk assessment
to individuals. Second, it means the government won't enable
us to diversify more broadly and at a reasonable cost. Third, it
encourages us all to deposit money in savings accounts at a time
when banks are paying little or no interest, leaving us exposed
to continuing high inflation. Fourth, given the banks' reluctance
to lend their deposits due to capital constraints, these proposals
inhibit the efficient allocation of our surplus cash to creditworthy
people and businesses.

While initiatives to improve financial advice are helpful, good
advice does not equate to simple investment products. The glacial
'Retail Distribution Review' will only alter compensation for
financial advisers from the end of 2012. Full advice will be fee-
based and therefore beyond most people. While advisers are
"considering" developing a simplified advice model that might
provide a "limited sales route", they claim to be worried that if
[when] investments do not perform customers may claim they
thought they were given full advice which proved to be wrong. I
wonder why?

In response to the sound of dragging feet, the government
commissioned the Consumer Financial Education Body to
develop a "free and impartial national advice service":

> "It will not give regulated advice, but it will provide people
> with information and advice on all major areas of money
> and personal finance. A key component of the national
> financial advice service will be a financial healthcheck, that
> will provide people with a holistic review of their finances,
> highlight areas to prioritise, and give people a personalised
> action plan to take forward. The service will move as close
> to the regulatory boundary as possible to ensure that people
> have a seamless journey between the national financial advice
> service and regulated advice, should they need it. To this end,
> CFEB is exploring the possibility of providing generic product

recommendations, for example '*you should consider purchasing home contents insurance*'."[163] [My italics.]

Hardly ambitious.

Loath as I am to admit that anything much comes from tinkering in Brussels, a little sunlight may penetrate via the 'key investor information document'[164] introduced at EU level to enable easier comparison of the key terms of multiple products. Professor Devlin also suggests that strong warnings on products that do not meet 'simple product' criteria and a traffic light system to declare the risk associated with them would help people make more suitable choices. He has urged the government to retain the rule that obliges a financial adviser to explain why any alternative product being recommended is at least as suitable as a simple product – a rule that led product providers to reduce fees for more complex products to make them at least as suitable as simple ones.

In October 2011, the government published a summary of the responses to its consultation on simple products,[165] and appointed a steering group "tasked with devising a suite of 'simple' financial products that will help consumers navigate the financial services market."

But why should I have to "navigate the financial services market" at all? Why aren't consumer finance products better aligned with consumers' day-to-day activities? I mean, why can't I put financial services in a shopping cart, like I can buy other stuff?

A better starting place for all financial services, not just 'simple products', is to consider the highly personalised, flexible ways in which people want to use money. As consumers, we don't think of money in terms of how it is regulated. We don't actually engage in 'banking', 'saving' or 'investing' as independent activities. Financial transactions are just steps (or hurdles) we encounter in the course of planning our retirement, heating our homes, educating our kids, buying a car or eating out. We expect to be able to use money to facilitate our activities – and to understand the cost – without expensive, complex, artificial barriers being placed in our way.

The reasons for the lack of simple retail financial products do not solely lie within retail banks' headquarters. That's why the

government has introduced a specific requirement for the new
FCA "to intervene in wholesale activity where this could be the
source of significant retail detriment", as mentioned at the start of
this chapter. Regulators must view all the financial markets – retail
and wholesale – not from the perspective of the institutions and
products they regulate, but in terms of what products are needed
downstream to enable consumers, SMEs and other customers to
use their money as they wish.

To achieve this requires a new, holistic approach to regulation.

Democratising the financial markets

One of President Obama's first acts on assuming office was to
berate Wall Street executives for taking the sixth largest round of
bonuses in history at taxpayers' expense. In doing so, he demonstrated not only the depth of public anger on the subject, but also
the massive scale of global regulatory failings. Since then, public
anger has surged to the point where citizens are rioting and striking against 'austerity measures'. Others have taken to occupying
major financial districts around the world in protest against the
excesses of the financial system.

This has all come about because our intensive investment and
securities regulations, ironically designed to protect the financial system and consumers, instead funnels all the world's major
investment funds and opportunities into a cloistered environment
in which a privileged few institutions are permitted to operate in a
way that suits themselves. As a direct result of that regime, those
institutions gain interest and other income from worldwide capital flows and can charge more or less whatever they like in fees, so
that enormous wealth accrues to their bottom lines, management
and staff. And that's just the 'traditional' regulated sector – there's
a much larger 'shadow banking' sector that regulators have largely
ignored until recently, which we'll examine shortly.

Here's an example of how poorly our regulations are aligned
with economic reality, even within the regulated sector.

In June 2010, the Office of Fair Trading announced its investigation into the alleged £2bn in fees charged by investment banks
for underwriting UK share issues – hardly their only income

producing activity. However, in its subsequent report, the OFT said that it would not refer that 'market' to the Competition Commission because major corporate clients and their institutional shareholders had only themselves to blame for the scale of the charges:

> "FTSE 350 companies raised an estimated £50bn of equity capital in the UK in 2009, paying around £1.4bn in fees, with average fees rising to more than 3% from around 2–2.5% in the period from 2003 to 2007. While such increases can be explained, in part, by stock market volatility during 2008 and early 2009… fees and discounts have been slow to fall in line with subsequent reductions in risk. …companies are generally not focused on the cost of equity underwriting services, instead prioritising speed, confidentiality and a successful 'take-up'. Some may also lack regular experience of raising equity capital which makes it difficult to hold investment banks to account on costs. *While institutional shareholders have expressed concerns about prices, they have yet to put sufficient pressure on companies to reduce the fees paid.*" [166] [My italics.]

This situation is a sign of gross market failure. Why don't investment bank clients and their institutional shareholders put pressure on investment banks to reduce fees? Is it because they all invest in each other and ultimately benefit from the revenues and profits? Is it because they know they can ultimately pass those fees on to retail investors, consumers and – when things take a turn for the worst – the taxpayers? We can add a big chunk of this £1.4bn in fees to the bail-outs, tax-free allowances and the giant spread between savings rates and loans already mentioned.

These are all line items in what it costs us to run our financial system, and we need those costs to come down fast.

Amidst the riots, strikes and tent cities the politicians and unelected technocrats haggling over the terms of sovereign bail-outs and bank recapitalisations barely seem to realise that the taxpayer now has a seat at the table. This new player demands to know how 'my money' is being used, and has the benefit of ever-increasing sunlight from traditional and social media focused on that very issue. This must lead to a serious reappraisal of the role of financiers and regulators alike. As Lord Turner, the chairman of the FSA, said in September 2009:

> "...[T]the top management of banks... need to operate within limits. *They need to be willing, like the regulator, to recognise that there are some profitable activities so unlikely to have a social benefit, direct or indirect, that they should voluntarily walk away from them.* They need to ask searching questions about whether the complex structured products they sold to corporate and institutional customers, truly did deliver real hedging value or simply encouraged those institutions into speculative and risky exposures which they did not understand: and, if the latter, they should not sell them even if they are profitable. They need to be willing to accept the capital and other requirements which will be imposed on activities of little value and considerable risk, rather than deploy lobbying power to argue against such constraints on the basis of a simplistic assertion that all innovation is always valuable."[167] [My italics.]

So the search must be on for ways in which our financial system can deliver the necessary social benefit – establish a genuine connection with the taxpayers and consumers.

One idea, amplified recently by Niall Ferguson[168] is to 'deleverage' the entire system by taking the losses necessary to rewrite consumer mortgages at more affordable rates. That may be a populist move that has an impact among those who have a mortgage. But such ideas assume support for leaving the financial system more or less as it was, with the focal point being 'zombie' banks that require on-going public support to make the necessary write-offs. And I don't believe there is the requisite public or political support for such a move.

Taxpayers know by now that they cannot ever safely turn their backs on finance again. Riots, strikes and the pitching of tents in the world's financial districts challenge the notion that matching investment capital and investment opportunities should be a rarefied activity reserved for the anointed few. The flipside must be a set of simplified, transparent marketplaces that are substantially open to all. Such a process of simplification, aimed at increased openness and transparency, would be entirely consistent with the rise of other directly accessible online consumer market-places during the past decade. In those market places, the role of the facilitator has been reduced to enabling consumers to seize control of their own experience and keep much more of the value previously retained by the 'old' packaged product providers. Indeed, we are already seeing the advent of such financial facilitators, in the form of peer-to-peer finance platforms. In this sense, the 'democratisation' of the financial markets may be seen as very much a natural, logical step, rather than anything terribly radical.

It will be important to get the rules right – just as that has been critical to the success of all the consumer platforms already out there. But openness, fairness, transparency – and taxpayers' determination to get out of this mess – ought to be reliable guides.

Of sunlight, shadow banking and horizontal intermediation

How did our financial system get into such a mess, right under the noses of the world's most aggressive financial regulators? In true 'Black Swan' tradition, this is something many have tried to rationalise by hindsight. But if we are to evolve a new, holistic approach to regulation, it is important to identify any obvious mistakes and try to learn something from them.

In July 2010, three years after the credit crisis dramatically surfaced, staff at the Federal Reserve Bank of New York finally claimed to have figured it out.[169] Their report came with a giant map which, as a leading financial journalist, Gillian Tett, observed:

> "...is a reminder of how clueless most investors, regulators and rating agencies were before 2007 about finance. After all, during the credit boom, there was plenty of research being conducted into the financial world; but I never saw anything remotely comparable to this road map."[170]

The NY Fed's report defines 'traditional banks' as depository institutions that are insulated by public sector insurance (read: taxpayers) from sudden 'runs' on their deposits. 'Shadow banks'

– finance companies, credit hedge funds, broker-dealers and an alphabet soup of intermediaries – are supposed to operate without any such public backing. Unfortunately, bail-out money *did* find its way to these 'shadow banks' because in many cases *they were part of the same corporate group as 'traditional banks'*.

In other words, the scale of financial activity that was actually being guaranteed by the taxpayer was a lot larger than the key officials and executives had ever realised. In fact, the NY Fed report shows that what we regarded as vast taxpayer bail-outs only reduced liabilities in the 'shadow banking system' from $20 trillion in March 2008 to about $16tn in Q1 2010. At that time, the liabilities in the traditional banking system were about $11tn.

Given this imbalance, shadow banking (especially the trade in unregulated derivatives) has been very much on the European regulatory agenda during the past few years. But these efforts have met fierce resistance from the affected firms which say the scope for unintended consequences is not well understood by legislators and regulators. That makes the publication of the NY Fed's report very much worthwhile. It concludes that "some" – but not all – segments of the shadow banking system are of "limited economic value". It says that "equally large segments of it have been driven by gains in specialisation" and would be more aptly described as a "parallel banking system." Nevertheless, the report concludes that "private sector balance sheets will always fail at internalising systemic risk [and] the official sector will always have to step in to help." So it's clear we are going to have to abandon the false distinction between regulated and unregulated financial activity.

How does the shadow banking system work?

Traditional banks use deposits to make loans and keep them, living off the interest and fee income, as well as re-lending it and paying (much less) interest to depositors. Such banks rely on numerous internal departments and business units to try to maximise the returns while minimising credit risk so that the bank remains a good or otherwise safe investment for its shareholders. Shadow banking generally involves making riskier loans than traditional banks, but selling them through a series of intermediaries (each a 'shadow bank') which act like the departments in a traditional bank to try to reduce the credit risk associated with the original loan so that it somehow becomes a good or safe investment. Each shadow bank specialises in one link in that "vertically integrated, long, intermediation chain". As the NY Fed explains:

> "These steps essentially amount to the 'vertical slicing' of traditional banks' credit intermediation process and include (1) loan origination, (2) loan warehousing, (3) [asset-backed security or ABS] issuance, (4) ABS warehousing, (5) ABS [collateralised debt obligation, or CDO] issuance, (6) ABS 'intermediation' and (7) wholesale funding...
>
> Typically, the poorer an underlying loan pool's quality at the beginning of the chain (for example a pool of sub-prime mortgages originated in California in 2006), the longer the credit intermediation chain that would be required to 'polish' the quality of the underlying loans to the standards of money market mutual funds and similar funds."

In reality, these chains could involve many more interim steps, (e.g. CDOs of CDOs, or 'CDOs squared'), depending on how many times the loans had to be 'polished'. Various charts in the NY Fed's report illustrate this eye-watering complexity very well.

Having studied shadow banking, the NY Fed believes that "regulation by function is a more potent style of regulation than regulation by institutional charter." Figuring out which functions contain the root cause of our current financial woes is therefore necessary. The NY Fed pins the blame for the credit crunch on the mis-pricing of 'ABS CDOs', (steps 5/6 in the above quote). This mis-pricing caused problems up and down the vertical chain. In essence, poor quality debt was repackaged again and again in order to remove the risk, but the risk was misunderstood and the resulting instruments were mis-priced each time they were sold.

Amazingly, notwithstanding these pricing problems, the NY Fed believes that 'vertical credit intermediation' is useful. It can reduce the costs of screening and monitoring borrowers in the traditional banking model, and facilitates investor diversification by transforming credit quality (i.e. splitting the repayments into some bonds that get paid before others), maturity dates (i.e.

making some bonds repayable earlier than the original loan) and adding liquidity (i.e. enabling bondholders' investment money to be used for making more loans). In addition, the NY Fed believes the grading of securities by a "credible rating agency" can better inform investors.

However, the events of the past decade have demonstrated that although vertical credit intermediation may be 'useful', it is not effective in managing credit risk. In fact, this model substantially increases the risk that instruments in the chain will be mis-priced. In particular, the mis-pricing of ABS CDOs demonstrates the flaw in the 'credible rating agency' model, which we'll explore shortly. And there are other challenges, not all of which were explicit in the report:

1. The separation of lender and borrower, and fragmentation of the original loan note makes it harder to undertake due diligence on large volumes of original loans, and to adjust those underlying loans when borrowers get into trouble (as is evident from the 'fraud closure' and 'forced repurchase' problems in the US).

2. The process of transforming 'maturity' (changing the date when loans or debt instruments are due to expire) creates balance sheet risk for the intermediary.

3. It is unclear whether ratings, accounting and audit functions really do remove information asymmetry between borrowers and lenders – hence the calls for reforms in these areas.

4. Pressure to reduce the amount of capital required to operate this vertical chain of intermediaries results in a game of regulatory, tax, capital and ratings arbitrage that spans the globe and creates endlessly complex corporate structures.

5. Various factors lead to underestimation of the capital required for the private and implicit public sector guarantees required to support it. This is further complicated by the fact that "...the performance of highly-rated structured securities... in a major liquidity crisis... becomes

highly correlated as all investors and funded institutions are forced to sell high quality assets in order to generate liquidity."

6   The knowledge that the market can ultimately 'put' problem securities on the taxpayer (whether this is explicit, implicit, direct or indirect) creates a moral hazard that seems to increase in line with the demand for the securities until the system irretrievably melts down.

These fundamental challenges and the length of time it is taking to confront them underscore the need to find alternatives to the vertical model for credit intermediation.

One such alternative is the horizontal model implemented by the peer-to-peer platforms that have sprung up since 2005. Taking the Zopa model as an example (since I helped create it), each borrower's total loan amount is made up of many £10 loans from many different lenders on the same technology platform at the start. So there's no need to split a single loan into many pieces later. None of the loan terms needs to be 'transformed' to enable lenders to achieve diversification across different loans, loan terms and borrowers. Lenders can spread their money in £10 units from the start. Zopa is not a party to the loan agreements made on its platform and segregates lenders' funds, so it has no credit risk (or 'balance sheet risk'), and therefore no need or temptation to engage in regulatory, tax or other arbitrage that banks and shadow banks attempt. The one-to-one legal relationship between borrower and loan owner is maintained for the life of each £10 loan via the same technology platform (with a back-up available), so all the data related to each loan is there for borrowers and lenders to see, and it's simple to assess the performance of the loan against its grade. To the extent that credit risk were to concentrate on certain borrowers or types of borrowers, those risks would remain visible, rather than rendered opaque through fragmentation, repackaging and re-grading of the underlying loans. Finally, the transparency and lack of balance sheet risk removes the scope for moral hazard.

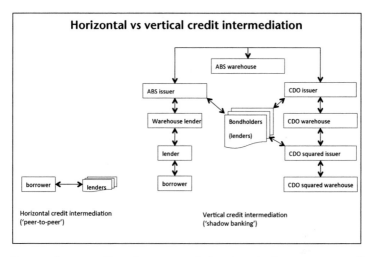

Loan volumes at Zopa have exceeded £160m to date – over 1% of the UK personal loan market – at an average default rate of less than 1%. Both lenders and borrowers achieve better rates on their savings and borrowing respectively than via traditional providers. Looking at the Zopa site on 15 November 2011, Zopa lenders had achieved an average return of 6.5% on money lent over the previous 12 months after a fee of 1% and before bad debt. Yet, as a peer-to-peer platform, Zopa remains unregulated under the current framework, and therefore the loans agreed on its platform do not qualify for money that is sheltered in people's tax-free allowances. That subsidised investment money goes to the usual suspects who, as we've seen, pay an average of 0.41% in interest and make a whopping 11% spread on savings and loans.

It's time that situation changed.

A new regulatory model for retail finance

Zopa may have been first to launch in March 2005, but a broad range of other peer-to-peer (P2P) finance platforms have since launched in the UK and in other countries. While substantial innovation in consumer and small business lending has been possible, UK rules against marketing investments like bonds, shares and unregulated collective investment schemes have made it much harder than necessary to offer alternative funding for individual consumers, start-ups, existing businesses and social projects. Given a more proportionate investment regime, the likes of Crowdcube, MarketInvoice and Buzzbnk would have started more quickly and cheaply, and might operate rather differently. They might also be joined by new P2P platforms as a substantial alternative to banks and other fee-hungry investment institutions, and distribute a range of financial instruments.

Oddly, given its reputation for fast-paced innovation, the US is even less supportive of alternative retail financial models. Zopa, for example, was unable to launch its P2P model in the US despite lengthy consultation with securities regulators. And life has been unnecessarily complicated for the likes of Prosper and Lending Club ever since.

To help remedy the regulatory imbalance, three of the leading UK commercial P2P platforms launched the Peer-to-Peer Finance Association (P2PFA) for platforms on which the majority of lenders and borrowers are consumers or small businesses, rather than, say, 'investment clubs' or networks of sophisticated investors. The P2PFA Operating Principles[171] are a set of self-regulatory measures based on members' existing terms and similar FSA requirements for payment services platforms (which have a similar, low risk profile). The principles require:

1   Senior management governance systems and controls;

2   Minimum amounts of capital;

3   Segregation of participants' funds;

4   Clear rules governing use of the platform, consistent with the Operating Principles;

5   Marketing and customer communications that are clear, fair and not misleading;

6   Secure and reliable IT systems;

7   Fair complaints handling; and

8   The orderly administration of contracts in the event a platform ceases to operate.

As at September 2011 there were three proposals in the US to allow peer-to-peer financing without requiring securities registration and unnecessarily onerous disclosures:

> "One petition, prepared in 2010 by the Sustainable Economies Law Center and, fittingly, paid for by a grass-roots crowd-funding effort, asks the SEC to permit entrepreneurs to raise up to $100 per individual and an aggregate of up to $100,000 without requiring expensive registration and disclosure.

> President Obama, as part of his jobs act, advocates an exemption for sums totalling up to $1m. Representative Patrick McHenry, a Republican from North Carolina, has drafted legislation that would allow companies to obtain up to $5m from individuals through crowdfunded ventures, with a cap of $10,000 per investor, or 10% of their annual incomes, whichever is smaller."[172]

In early November 2011, the US House of Representative passed a bill (still subject to Senate and Presidential approval) which would allow an issuer to raise small amounts of money from many people (crowdfunding) on the following basis:

- "The [issuer] may only raise a maximum of $1m, or $2m if the [issuer] provides potential investors with audited financial statements;

- Each investor is limited to investing an amount equal to the lesser of (i) $10,000 or (ii) 10% of his or her annual income;

- The issuer or the intermediary, if applicable, must take a number of steps to limit the risk to investors, including (i) warning them of the speculative nature of the investment and the limitations on resale, (ii) requiring them to answer questions demonstrating their understanding of the risks, and (iii) providing notice to the SEC of the offering, including certain prescribed information."[173]

Would these proposals work in practice?

Absolutely. The challenge (and benefit) associated with such 'safe harbours' is that there is very little room for fee income. This in turn favours 'thin intermediaries', like P2P and other electronic finance platforms, as a means of open, horizontal distribution, as described above. Proportionately regulating such platforms to address horizontal issues like those covered by the P2PFA Operating Principles leverages economies of scale, leaving product providers to focus purely on instrument-specific requirements.

Under this regulatory model, the platforms can control operational risk; guard against money laundering; deliver transparency through adequate product disclosure and 'my account' functionality; and centralise customer service and complaints handling, with ultimate referral to financial ombudsmen or other complaints handling bodies.

In addition, because the platforms provide a reliable audit trail, they would enable the government to expand tax-free investment incentives to encompass the instruments traded on them. This would improve investors' ability to diversify, and enable the re-allocation of the currently passive tax-free investment money to creditworthy people and businesses that need it. Similarly, tax rules should permit losses to be offset against gains and income derived via such platform-related activity outside tax shelters, as they do regulated assets.

Moreover, by enabling the efficient use of technology to facilitate consumers' desire for greater personal control, governments will be helping to build a decent, sustainable financial services industry.

---

131 Including a post at The Fine Print, my legal blog (or 'blawg'): http://sdj-thefine-print.blogspot.com/

132 http://www.ft.com/cms/s/0/cf7d4f6e-e533-11df-8e0d-00144feabdc0.html

133 http://www.breakingviews.com/enrons-worst-legacy-auditors-too-big-to-fail/1613021.article

134 http://www.accountancyage.com/aa/news/1808799/kpmg-considered-entering-credit-rating-market

135 http://ec.europa.eu/commission_2010-2014/barnier/headlines/news/2011/11/20111111_en.htm

136 http://www.sec.gov/news/press/2008/2008-211.htm

137 http://www.blogger.com/www.ft.com/cms/s/0/dfd9ed06-0d31-11e0-82ff-00144feabdc0.html

138 http://www.fsa.gov.uk/pages/Library/Communication/PR/2010/062.shtml

139 http://www.ft.com/cms/s/0/9ca9a0b0-0c3e-11e0-b1a3-00144feabdc0.
html#axzz18kO3DHM4
140 http://www.ft.com/cms/s/0/da54e942-0c6b-11e0-8408-00144feabdc0.html
141 http://www.jampartners.com/site_equity/inv_team.asp. Quoted in The Big
Short.
142 See Financial Services and Markets Tribunal decision concerning Legal and General's Flexible Mortgage Plans.
143 'Metaphors, Models and Theories' http://papers.ssrn.com/sol3/papers.cfm?
abstract_id=1713405
144 http://media.ft.com/cms/9e73f678-fb1d-11dc-8c3e-000077b07658.pdf; The Bank
of England will be responsible for protecting the stability of the financial system
as a whole (via its Financial Policy Committee (FPC)), and will supervise deposit
takers, insurers and significant investment firms (via its Prudential Regulation
Authority (PRA)). A new Financial Conduct Authority (FCA) will be responsible
for regulating conduct in retail and wholesale markets, supervising the trading
infrastructure that supports those markets; and for the prudential regulation of
firms not regulated by the PRA.
145 http://www.fsa.gov.uk/pubs/events/fca_approach.pdf, Chapter 5.
146 http://www.fsa.gov.uk/pubs/events/fca_approach.pdf, Chapter 5.
147 http://www.bankingcode.org.uk/pdfdocs/Bulletin%2031.pdf.
148 A decision is due in late 2011 (http://www.hm-treasury.gov.uk/consult_consum-
er_credit.htm).
149 http://www.berr.gov.uk/files/file52072.pdf
150 http://sdj-pragmatist.blogspot.com/2010/12/magic-of-madoff.html
151 http://www.fs-cp.org.uk/newsroom/2010/157.shtml
152 http://www.nao.org.uk/publications/1011/support_for_banks.aspx
153 http://www.cimetric.co.uk/TISA%20ISA%20Report%202011%20Executive%20
Summary_synopsis.pdf
154 http://blog.zopa.com/archives/2011/09/16/mori-research-on-bank-spreads/
155 http://www.oft.gov.uk/news-and-updates/press/2008/84-08
156 http://www.oft.gov.uk/news/press/2008/84-08
157 http://www.cps.org.uk/cps_catalog/simplification%20is%20the%20key%20
%28reduced%29.pdf
158 http://www.hm-treasury.gov.uk/d/lessons_learned_from_simple_products_ini-
tiatives.pdf ('Devlin')
159 http://www.hm-treasury.gov.uk/d/simple_financial_products_consultation.pdf,
(para 2.13)
160 http://www.natcen.ac.uk/media/606958/nat%20british%20social%20atti-
tudes%20survey%20summary%206.pdf
161 http://ec.europa.eu/consumers/strategy/docs/4th_edition_scoreboard_en.pdf
162 http://www.hm-treasury.gov.uk/consult_simple_financial_products.htm
163 HMT, para 4.3; see also Devlin, p.29
164 http://www.cesr-eu.org/index.php?page=consultation_details&id=170
165 http://www.hm-treasury.gov.uk/press_116_11.htm
166 http://www.oft.gov.uk/news-and-updates/press/2011/08-11
167 http://www.fsa.gov.uk/pages/Library/Communication/Speeches/2009/0922_
at.shtml

168 http://www.ft.com/cms/s/0/85106daa-f140-11dd-8790-0000779fd2ac.html?nclick_check=1
169 http://www.ny.frb.org/research/staff_reports/sr458.pdf
170 http://www.ft.com/cms/s/0/1a222bf4-f33d-11df-a4fa-00144feab49a.html#axzz15krnmRPW
171 http://www.p2pfinanceassociation.org.uk/rules-and-operating-principles
172 http://www.nytimes.com/2011/09/26/opinion/a-proposal-to-allow-small-private-companies-to-get-investors-online.html
173 http://venturebeat.com/2011/11/08/faq-what-the-new-u-s-crowdfunding-bill-means-for-entrepreneurs/

Lightning Source UK Ltd.
Milton Keynes UK
UKOW052207090112

185033UK00001B/41/P